my life, unscripted

By Tricia Goyer

THOMAS NELSON
Since

NASHVILLE   DALLAS   MEXICO CITY   RIO DE JANEIRO   BEIJING

To Leslie Joy

Yes, Joy is your middle name,
and the life-script you're writing brings
those who know you much joy.
Keep seeking Him.

Published in Nashville, Tennessee, by Thomas Nelson. Thomas Nelson is a trademark of Thomas Nelson, Inc.

Thomas Nelson, Inc., titles may be purchased in bulk for educational, business, fund-raising, or sales promotional use. For information, please e-mail SpecialMarkets@ThomasNelson.com.

Unless otherwise noted, Scripture quotations are taken from the HOLY BIBLE, NEW INTERNATIONAL VERSION®. © 1973, 1978, 1984 by International Bible Society. Used by permission of Zondervan Publishing House. All rights reserved. Scripture quotations marked (AMP) are taken from the Amplified® Bible, © 1954, 1958, 1962, 1964, 1965, 1987 by The Lockman Foundation. Used by permission. Scripture quotations marked (THE MESSAGE) are taken from The Message by Eugene H. Peterson. © 1993, 1994, 1995, 1996, 2000, 2001, 2002. Used by permission of NavPress Publishing Group. All rights reserved. Scripture quotations marked (NKJV) are taken from the New King James Version. © 1979, 1980, 1982, Thomas Nelson, Inc. Used by permission. All rights reserved. Scripture quotations marked (NLT) are taken from the Holy Bible, New Living Translation, © 1996. Used by permission of Tyndale House Publishers, Inc., Wheaton, Illinois 60188. All rights reserved.

Library of Congress Cataloging-in-Publication Data

Goyer, Tricia.
    My life, unscripted : who's writing your life / by Tricia Goyer.
        p. cm.
    Includes bibliographical references and index.
    ISBN-10: 1-4003-1052-0 (trade paper)
    ISBN-13: 978-1-4003-1052-4 (trade paper)
    1. Teenagers—Religious life. 2. Self-actualization (Psychology)—Religious aspects—Christianity. I. Title.
    BV4531.3.G69 2007
    248.8'3—dc22

                                        2007013451

Printed in the United States of America
07 08 09 10 11 RRD 9 8 7 6 5 4 3 2 1

Contents

Contents

Lights, Camera . . .
Action!
(a note about this book)

My Life, Unscripted may look a little different from other books you've seen. For one, there are actual scripts within the book. Some of them are ones I've made up. Others are true scenes from my life that I've written out in script form.

I've tried to make these scripts as real-to-life as possible. I've designed these to look like they would if they were in the hands of a director.

In writing these scripts, I've used the same terminology as a scriptwriter. Here are a few terms you might come across:

TERMS

Establishing: (Establishing shot) An image or shot that indicates the location of the scene and/or story.

Ext.: (Exterior) Used in the scene heading, this indicates that the scene is taking place outdoors.

Fade In: (Fade from black) When an image slowly appears from black. This is typically used at the beginning of a film. Sometimes it is used between scenes to show time passing between points in the story.

Fade Out: (Fade to black) When an image slowly disappears into black. This is typically used at the end of a scene.

Int.: (Interior) Used in the scene heading, this indicates that the scene is taking place indoors.

CAPS: You will also note that certain words are in all CAPS. This is not a mistake!

In the beginning of each section, each NEW PERSON OR GROUP OF PEOPLE will be in ALL CAPS. This is a cue for the casting director. It tells him the number of people he will need to cast.

Also, each SOUND is in ALL CAPS. This helps the soundman to know which sounds will be needed for the scene.

Pretty interesting stuff, isn't it?

And for my own personal touch, you'll see that the Scriptures are in the same font as the scripts . . . because here in the real world, these Scriptures should be the *script* for our lives.

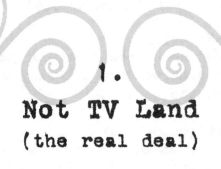

1.

Not TV Land
(the real deal)

If you were to come across the script for a new (and just a bit cheesy) teen movie, the script might be written something like this:

FADE IN:

EXT. HIGH SCHOOL FOOTBALL GAME—NIGHT—ESTABLISHING

Stadium stands filled with CHEERING FANS. SCHOOL BAND plays SCHOOL SONG as FOOTBALL PLAYERS run onto field.

INT. CAR IN PARKING LOT—NIGHT

Soda cans and fast-food wrappers littering the floor are KICKED aside by trendy shoes belonging to MEGAN JOHNSON, 16. Light from the stadium filters through the back window over the muscled, tan body of CHRIS COOPER. He brushes Megan's hair from her cheek and turns Megan's face toward him.

> **CHRIS**
> You don't have to be shy, Meg.
> We've been talking about this all week.

my life, unscripted

> **MEGAN** (wryly)
> Talked about the football game, yes.
> I thought we were actually going to
> watch the game.

> **CHRIS** (chuckling)
> And why would I do that when I have
> the most beautiful girl in school
> right here? Besides, I don't even
> like sports.

Megan OPENS DOOR and climbs from car.

> **MEGAN**
> Chris, I came to watch the game, not
> fend off your plays.

Megan slips her purse over her shoulder and
steps back from the car. She SLAMS the door
shut. Chris LOWERS THE AUTOMATIC WINDOW.

> **CHRIS** (stuttering)
> But I thought . . .

> **MEGAN**
> I know exactly what you thought.
> Sorry, Chris, no touchdown tonight.

Chris STARTS THE ENGINE.

> **CHRIS**
> Yeah, well, you're not the only girl
> in this school. . . .

Megan watches Chris drive away.

MEGAN
I know. But I am the only one who has
to live with the consequences. . . .

FADE OUT

A TYPICAL MOVIE?

Now that would make a typical movie, right? We'd watch as Meg goes to the football game shaken, but proud to have dumped the creep. If it were a great movie, Meg would meet a cute guy sitting in the bleachers. Of course, then there would be some conflict that keeps them apart. Maybe he's rich, and she's poor. Maybe he's a rich prince from Denmark! Oh wait, that's been done. Maybe his parents have big plans for him, which don't include her. Maybe hers are shipping Meg to boarding school.

But no matter the conflict, in the end they confess their love. And though the movie only ends with a kiss, we know their happiness lasts forever.

Ahhh . . .

Unfortunately, the script of my life went a little more like this:

FADE IN:

**EXT. FAMILY SEDAN DRIVING DOWN ROAD IN
SMALL TOWN—AFTERNOON—ESTABLISHING
INT. CAR CARRIES MOM AND DAUGHTER—AFTERNOON**

Tears run down MOM'S face. Her jaw is clenched tight. In the passenger seat, TRISH VALLEY, 17, slumps lower into the seat. She wipes away her own tears and wraps her arms around her waist almost instinctively. Her eyes widen as a car passes. Driving the beat-up Ford is a teen boy. A PRETTY GIRL rides with CHASE, 16, curled to his side. Trish sits straight and points to the car.

> **TRISH**
> There he is. Follow him.
>
> **MOM** (surprised)
> Are you sure? Do you want me to turn around?
>
> **TRISH** (hurriedly)
> Yes. Turn around.

The sedan turns and follows the Ford to the McDonald's parking lot. Trish jumps from her car, SLAMS the door, and stalks to the Ford. Her eyes refuse to meet those of the girl in the passenger's seat. She focuses her eyes on the boy.

> **TRISH** (angrily)
> We need to talk.
>
> **CHASE** (annoyed)
> Now?

> **TRISH** (with quivering voice)
> Yes, now.

Trish stalks toward the large trash can at the corner of the parking lot. Chase follows. She pauses and turns to him. His gaze is ice cold. Trish's hands are shaking as she crosses her arms over her chest and takes a deep breath.

> **TRISH**
> I'm pregnant.

> **CHASE**
> I don't believe you.

> **TRISH**
> It doesn't matter what you believe or don't believe. I am pregnant.

> **CHASE**
> So what are you going to do?

> **TRISH**
> I'm going to, uh, have a baby.

> **CHASE**
> What about like last time?

> **TRISH** (hurt)
> An abortion?

Trish lowers her gaze, then shakes her head.

TRISH
I'm not doing that again. I'm having
this baby.

CHASE
I doubt it's even mine.

TRISH (hurt)
Whatever. I don't need you.

Trish stalks away, then she glances back
over her shoulder. She watches Chase
saunter to his car and to the other girl.

FADE OUT

MY SCRIPT

A little different script, don't you think? Of course, the first
script is something I imagined. The second is a scene I've
lived through.

Writing the scene I starred in (even a number of years
after the fact) causes a surge of emotions. Anger at my former
boyfriend—yes, even after all these years. Anger at myself for
being *sooooo* stupid to get myself into that situation. (That
situation and many others. As you'll read within the pages of
this book, more than one scene from my life played out like
a bad teen movie.)

Writing that scene also brought relief that I'm no longer
that person, along with hints of joy that God has done so
much with my life.

But more than anything, as I look back at my drama-filled teen years, I wonder . . . *What was I thinking?*

The truth? I wasn't. I lived from day to day on **every wave of emotion** I experienced. On some days excitement and passion partnered up, pattering wildly within my heart. Other days, depression and anxiety were my silent friends. I lived each day as it came, with no plan for my future, for my relationships, or for my heart. I lived my life completely unscripted . . . and, *well,* you saw how well that went for me.

How about you? What type of script are you writing for your life?

When I say "script" I'm not talking about career goals or college plans. I'm not talking about current class schedules or finding the unique purpose for your future. While all of those are important, there are other parts of our life we need to script, too, such as:

- Dealing with peer pressure from both guys and friends.

- The search for popularity. How to find it. Or live without. Or be happy in between.

- Relationships with parents. No matter how out of touch with reality they seem to be.

- And living for God without turning your back on the world.

Scripting your life comes down to thinking through struggles—yours as well as the struggles of others—and considering the best approach. While there are dozens of teen books and magazines out there dealing with these relationship-type topics, I'm going to lay it all out there by (1) sharing my past experiences (which would be easier and more comfortable to hide), (2) including input from teens just like you, and

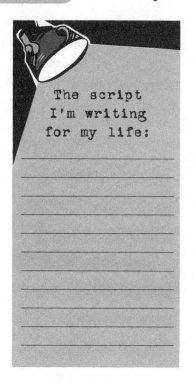

The script
I'm writing
for my life:

_____

_____

_____

_____

_____

_____

_____

_____

_____

_____

_____

(3) showing God's POV (point of view), through God's Word—the Bible. We'll dig deep to uncover answers concerning our lives and our place in the world.

Why use the Bible? According to a recent survey, "Almost two-thirds of teens (62 percent) believe that the Bible is totally accurate in all of its teachings."[1] If you're part of this majority, then you'll already appreciate how God's Word can help you in everyday life. If you aren't sure how you feel about the Bible, feel free to stick around and keep an open mind. Humor me if you will.

Scene Change

Personally, God's Word and God's people turned *my* life around. You see, the Trish Valley script you read earlier wasn't just partly true—it was exactly as I remember it.

After that awful scene, my boyfriend dumped me for good, and I dropped out of my senior year of high school. (It was too hard going to school—seeing him with someone else, *and* dealing with my own issues/mistakes/emotions too.) I decided to have my baby, especially since I was dealing with the heartache and regret of a previous abortion. And as my stomach grew, I became more and more depressed.

Unlike some mistakes, an unplanned pregnancy is not one you can hide very easily. Each day I walked around with the evidence sticking out before me like a basketball under my shirt.

During that painful time, I decided to give God another chance. I'd grown up in church, but during my teen years, decided I wanted to do my own thing. And when "my own thing" left me sad and alone, my grandma's Bible study group invited me to join them. These sweet old ladies also welcomed me to church and threw me a baby shower (while my teen friends dropped out of the picture). These women showed me what the love of God is all about.

And it was during one of my depressing days, when I was six months pregnant and feeling abandoned by both my boyfriend and friends, I gave my heart to the Lord. I told Him, "God, I've completely screwed up my life this time. If You can do better, please do so." It wasn't a fancy prayer, but it worked.

My Script:

Well, first of all, my life is not nearly as exciting as a TV sitcom's stars.' Second of all, my life is real. It isn't staged, and I have to deal with things without a script telling me what to do. When problems arise, I must deal with them, and unfortunately, they aren't always solved within a thirty-minute time frame.
—Melanie, Texas, age 17

Sometimes I think through situations. Sometimes I don't. I mean, life isn't going to always turn out the way you think it's going to . . . but then again, if you don't think out some things it can be a catastrophe.
—Leslie, Montana, age 14

Now you might be scratching your head and wondering what type of book this is. Don't worry. It's not a book about teen pregnancy, and I'm not going to spend the next twenty chapters sharing my story. Instead, it's a book designed to help you think through some of life's hardest challenges:

My Script:

Although we all have many problems every day, be it Christianity, boys, school, etc., the people on TV shows don't usually face real-life situations and almost always seem to choose the option more likely to get them into trouble instead of taking responsibility for themselves.
—Jayme, Montana, age 12

On TV everything works out great, perfect. Everything. My life often doesn't.
—Hannah, Ohio, age 13

- The people you interact with every day
- Your inner longings to be different, better, unique
- And even your interaction with a world that may not know your name, but often dictates how you feel about yourself

As you've witnessed, I'm not someone who comes to you with a testimony of perfection. I hope you make different choices than I did. But maybe reading through some of my life "scripts" can help you choose better ones for yourself. And help you work with whatever scenes you've already lived out and now regret.

You see, we all mess up one time or another. Yet I have good news. If God proved to have big plans for a former pregnant, teen dropout, you can be certain He has good plans for you too!

Your life may not be anything like what you see on television or at the movies. And I hope you wouldn't want it to be. TV Land is not reality, and every situation that comes your way isn't over in thirty minutes with a happy conclusion.

Real life is different, but it's also better. Especially when we look to God to help us with life as we know it. Ready to get started?

Lights, camera . . . reality!

Intermission

sto·ry·board *noun.* a panel or panels on which a sequence of sketches depicts the significant changes of action and scene in a planned film, as for a movie, television show, or advertisement.[2]

Studios use storyboards to provide an easy way to follow the sequence of a story. They can use illustrations, photos, or words to sketch a series of events. Now you can use this too. Take time to storyboard your life in the empty boxes below. Note significant events, like:

- The hardest thing you've faced in life
- What you most regret
- A time you felt really upset
- One of your favorite memories

And others . . . If you were to make a movie of YOU this far—what events would you include?

Did you sketch some of your favorite moments? You also might have come up with some sad times. Or times when, like me, you really screwed up.

Now, I want you to review the frames (boxes) and consider that Jesus was there with you during each event. Can you see the smile on His face during those joyous moments? Or can you imagine Him crying with you? And even during those times when you screwed up, take time to picture Jesus by your side, ready and waiting for you to turn to Him. In fact, He's still waiting now.

If there are times from your past—whether from five years or five minutes ago—that you regret, understand Jesus is willing to forgive you now. Romans 3:23 says, **"For all have sinned and fall short of the glory of God."** No one has a perfect storyboard!

In the back of the book you'll find "Giving Your Life to Jesus." If you haven't already done this, check it out. If you have, then you understand how accepting the **forgiveness of God** is *the* key event in your storyboard.

The word *forgiveness* actually means "to send away." Give Jesus your regrets, and He'll cast them away, like someone throwing out a filthy, stinky, old pair of sweaty socks. In return, Jesus offers His purity and peace, wrapping His righteousness around you like a pure white robe. Your memories won't disappear overnight, but in God's eyes it will be as if those events never happened.

It's a good feeling. I know. I remember what it was like. At age seventeen, when I asked Jesus to cast away my sin, I was still pregnant, in need of friends, and had to face many consequences of my actions, but a new emotion overwhelmed me. **Hope.** It was the wonderful feeling of a real God touching down on *my* reality.

It wasn't TV Land. It was better.

2.

Dialogue
(the way you talk to yourself)

di·a·logue *noun.* 1. a conversation
between two persons. 2. the lines spoken
by characters in drama or fiction.[1]

What do you say when you talk to yourself? No, I'm serious. What do you say?

Whether we know it or not, there is a continual dialogue going through our minds. The dialogue occurs in two ways:

1. **Unscripted**: Out-of-control, spontaneous, unanchored. It's when your social calendar, the people around you, and whatever emotion of the day or hour takes over and rules your life.

2. **Scripted**: A solid plan. It's something YOU create after thinking through situations, considering your plans and what you want, talking to God about your worries, cares, and hopes. Then you actively determine how to handle life (with God's help and strength). So even when everything feels whacked out, you have something solid to hold on to.

Unfortunately, during my teen years, I didn't have any idea it was possible to script my thoughts. I learned quickly that how I thought was what I believed. And what I believed,

Things I tell
myself:

_____
_____
_____
_____
_____
_____
_____
_____
_____
_____

I lived. And living with my emotions just millimeters from the surface didn't always make a pretty picture.

FADE IN:

EXT. HIGH SCHOOL STADIUM—NIGHT— ESTABLISHING

Football game. FANS piling into cars with huge grins. Winning TEAM runs back to locker room. A SMALL CLUSTER OF PEOPLE— PARENTS, FRIENDS, and GIRLFRIENDS—wait outside locker room for victorious football players to reemerge.

Striding up to the group is TRISH VALLEY, 16, still wearing her cheerleading uniform from that night's game. Instead of excitement over the win, her eyes narrow when she spots ALEXIS, the girl CHASE cheated with just last week. Alexis glances to Trish and smiles, turning back toward the locker room. Trish strides toward her.

  TRISH
What are you doing here?

  ALEXIS (snotty)
Waiting for Chase, of course.

TRISH (angrily)
Chase said you two broke up.

ALEXIS
That's not what he told me last
night.

TRISH
You little . . .

Trish throws her pom-poms in Alexis's
face. Her fists follow. Both are swinging
blows. The crowd of onlookers CALL OUT and
breaks them up. Chase runs out of locker
room toward Trish.

CHASE
What's going on?

TRISH
What does it look like? You said
you weren't seeing her anymore.

CHASE
I'm not.

TRISH
That's not what she said.

CHASE
I told her I'd talk to her tonight,
after the game. To break things off.

TRISH
Forget it. This isn't worth it. It's over.

CHASE
That's what you said last time.

TRISH
This time I mean it. . . .

Chase reaches a hand to Trish's face.

CHASE
Your lip is bleeding.

Trish picks up her pom-poms from the ground. From the corner of her eye she spots Alexis CRYING with a group of her friends gathered around.

TRISH (mumbling to herself)
Who cares about my lip? What's really bleeding is my heart.

FADE OUT

YOUR INNER DIALOGUE
(THAT LITTLE VOICE IN YOUR MIND)

The dialogue you play and replay in your mind will come out in your actions. During this time in my life, one message I believed was that Chase was the only guy for me. I also believed we would be happy together if it weren't for these *other people* who kept getting in the way.

Instead of realizing what a messed up relationship I was in, I took it out on everyone else. The voices in my head also told me that if I was better, prettier, more caring, etc., then my boyfriend wouldn't stray.

How about you? What does your current, internal dialogue involve? Your thoughts will control your beliefs—which, in turn, will control your actions. This may not result in throwing punches . . . although that is a real possibility.

Believe it or not, you don't have to leave your life (thoughts, beliefs, actions) to chance. You don't have to be caught up in the drama, pulled along by every new character that pops into the scenes of your life (whether positively or negatively). Instead, you can realize you *are* the Star Performer in your life story. You can write the script.

Being the Star Performer of your world doesn't mean you're the center of the universe, but rather you understand that God—who *is* the center of the universe—created you with *a role to play*. Not only that, He's provided His Word (the Script) and the Holy Spirit (the Internal Director) to guide you along the way.

To live life *scripted* means to allow God's Word to guide your thoughts, actions, emotions, and desires *before* you throw yourself into the drama of life.

To see how this works in real life, let's use the above example of Trish Valley . . . which is another scene from my life that is regrettably true.

First, let's start by talking about some of the lies I believed during this time:

- I needed a guy's love. Or rather *this* guy's love.
- Other people were the problem.
- I had to fight for what I wanted.

Instead of allowing my emotions to rule my actions, what if I had taken time to consider God's plans and thoughts for *me*? Today, one of my favorite Scriptures is Psalm 139:14–17 (THE MESSAGE). This is what it says:

You know exactly how I was made, bit by bit,
how I was sculpted from nothing into
something.
Like an open book, you watched me grow from
conception to birth;
All the stages of my life were spread out
before you,
The days of my life all prepared
before I'd even lived one day.
Your thoughts—how rare, how beautiful!
God, I'll never comprehend them!

Personally, I think my beliefs would have been a little bit different if I would have filled my mind with this dialogue.

God sculpted me . . . which means He created me just as He wanted. I am good enough for *His* plans. No, wait. With God it's always *best*. I am *best* for His plans.

God prepared all the days of my life. Did He plan for heartache from bad relationships, or did I bring that on myself? (I'd guess the latter.)

God's thoughts of me are rare and beautiful. Why would I believe anything less? Or let others think any less of me?

Lately, my
thinking has
led to:

Our lives are radically changed when we replace our internal dialogue with the truth of God's Word. In *your* everyday life, the best way to check your internal dialogue is to see if it matches up with God's truth. If it doesn't, it's a lie, and it's not from God. And if you're listening to these lies, then your beliefs and actions will follow them rather than God's good plans.

Throwing punches was just one of the actions that resulted

from my wrong thinking. This is just one way bad dialogue shows up in its lived-out form. What about you? Where has your thinking got you lately?

Intermission

stage di·rec·tion noun.
1. an instruction written into the script of a play, indicating stage actions, movements of performers, or production requirements.
2. the art or technique of a stage director.[2]

Try to picture a TV show or a movie in which no stage direction is given. Or rather, the stage direction is given, but no one listens. The director knows what he's trying to accomplish, but instead everyone decides *their own way* is best. What a mess!

The same is true when we attempt to follow our own plans instead of God's in everyday life. Personally, as I've spent time with God over the years, I've come to a few brilliant observations:

My Script:

When it comes to God playing a part in my life, it's not as much as I want Him to. Actually not that much at all.
—Maddie, California, age 15

The drama in my life is probably the most distracting to my relationship with God. I realized earlier this year that if I let drama be more important in my life than God, I will get nowhere.
—Sarah, Minnesota, age 14

I know that God should be making an impact on my life, and He does, but sometimes it just seems like He isn't there.
—Jayme, Montana, age 12

YOU can't force yourself to want a better relationship with God, but God can help. If you seek Him, He will give you a desire for a relationship. It's really hard sometimes, but it always turns out for the best.
—Sarah, Colorado, age 15

- God knows all.
- God has a great plan.
- God loves me more than anyone else ever could.

Hmmm . . . maybe it would be wise to listen up, and tune in to what this plan is all about.

One of the biblical writers came to the same conclusion. In Romans 3:27–28 (THE MESSAGE) we read:

> What we've learned is this: God does not respond to what we do; we respond to what God does. We've finally figured it out. Our lives get in step with God and all others by letting him set the pace, not by proudly or anxiously trying to run the parade.

The best way to figure out God's stage directions is to read His Word. Throughout my life, I've gone about this different ways.

Sometimes I choose one book of the Bible and read through it a few times, pausing to consider main thoughts.

Other times I set a schedule such as reading one to two chapters a day. Then, every day, I write down my favorite verses in a notebook.

Sometimes I find verses throughout Scripture that fit a specific theme, such as forgiveness, hope, peace, etc.

Below is an example of this last method. I've decided to go with the theme "God's Thoughts and God's Plans" since that's what we're talking about.

4U2 Try:

1. Take time to look up the following Scriptures.
2. In the space provided, jot down your thoughts of these verses.
3. Finally, answer this question: **How would my thoughts, beliefs, and actions change if I trusted these verses were truth?**

Isaiah 55:8–12

Psalm 33:11

Psalm 40:5

Isaiah 46:10

Hosea 14:9

3.

Character Sketches

(all about you)

char·ac·ter sketch *noun.* a brief description of a
person's qualities.[1]

When a scriptwriter starts working on a new story, one of the
first things he maps out is the character. Not only what the character looks like, but how the person will think, feel, and react.

When writing a novel or screenplay, the author asks,
What is my character's main motivation? Another way to ask
this is to consider: *What does he or she want more than anything in the world?*

After considering this, the writer begins the story. The
things that stand in the character's way for getting what he or
she wants is the *conflict* of the novel. Then, by the end of the
story, the writer either: (1) helps the character overcome
problems or obstacles to reach the goal, or (2) has the character reach a different goal . . . but one in which the character decides is exactly what she wanted after all, but just
didn't know it.

Through the course of the story, the character is someone
we love and root for. We cheer her on and encourage her to
keep going, no matter what obstacles get in her way.

When it comes to writing stories, it's up to the writer to figure out the characteristics of the story's hero. It's also up to the
writer to figure out the character's motivation. When it comes
to your life, your character and motivation are up to you.

24

FADE IN:

INT. SCHOOL CLASSROOM—DAY—ESTABLISHING

STUDENTS sitting in desks, TALKING amongst themselves. TEACHER handing back essays. The BELL RINGS. Students file out of room, except one female student.

What is my motivation? What do I want more than anything in the world?

_____

_____

_____

_____

TRISH VALLEY, 15, stays in her seat. When the last student has exited, she slowly turns over her paper and smiles at the A. Hesitantly, she walks up to the teacher's desk. Trish CLEARS HER THROAT and the teacher, Mr. Duncan, looks up.

> **TRISH**
> Um, Mr. Duncan? Last month you passed out information on the American Legion Essay contest. . . . Do you think my essay would be a good fit?

> **MR. DUNCAN** (distracted)
> Oh, yes, you got an _A_, right? Sure. Why don't you talk to Mrs. Alexander about that? I'm not organizing the essays this year.

> **TRISH** (shyly)
> Uh, okay. If you think it's a good fit.

> **MR. DUNCAN**
> Sure, just tell Mrs. Alexander I
> gave the okay.

Trish makes her way to MRS. ALEXANDER'S
room. She sees the OLDER STUDENTS arriving
for the next class.

> **TRISH** (mumbling)
> I didn't stay up three nights in a
> row writing this thing for nothing
> . . . might as well try.

Trish pauses in the doorway, and then she
enters and walks toward the teacher. Mrs.
Alexander looks up from her desk. The BELL
RINGS, but she ignores it.

> **MRS. ALEXANDER**
> Can I help you? Are you a new student?

> **TRISH**
> No. I, uh, have an essay for the
> contest. Mr. Duncan sent me down.

Mrs. Alexander takes the paper without
looking at it.

> **MRS. ALEXANDER**
> Okay, I'll submit it. Now you better
> hurry; you're already tardy for your
> next class.

Trish hurries from the room, and she is
sure she hears RUDE CHUCKLES from the

older students. She races down the hall, and she chides herself for taking the essay to Mrs. Alexander.

TRISH
What was I thinking? It's not like I'll win, anyway. Now I'm going to have a tardy. . . .

FADE OUT

BELIEVING IN YOURSELF

Have you ever been in this situation? Did you ever believe in yourself and your abilities, only to find you were the only one who did?

When I was in high school, I loved to read and write. I got good grades in English, but when it came to getting praise from my parents, or my teachers, it seemed no one else cared about my writing as much as I did.

"It's good, dear. Nice job," I often heard, but no one took the time to encourage me, much less push me to do better.

There were times when I went out of my way to sign up for a writing contest or to read an extra-credit book. But after a while I wondered why I was doing it. No one seemed to notice or care. Why should I?

In fact, the scene above is true. I asked to enter my essay in the contest, and the teacher put it in the stack with the others. Though neither teacher seemed to give much thought to it, in the end I won second place in our county! It was a nice reminder that rooting for myself—being my biggest fan, even when others didn't seem to notice—was worth the effort.

Yet, unfortunately, that was one of only a few times I took a stand for myself. I hate to think of how many other opportunities I missed. It was easier to pretend writing didn't matter. It was easier to put down the book I was reading to do silly things with my friends, rather than appearing "different." Overall, during my high school years, I didn't trust myself enough to follow my dreams hidden deep inside. I found it easier to go along with the crowd than to consider my unique characteristics, dreams, and goals.

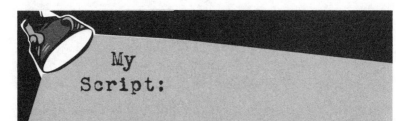

My Script:

Sometimes I feel like I am playing a part. I feel like if I act (or don't act) a certain way in front of others they will think badly of me.
—Ashley, Pennsylvania, age 17

I try to be real with people and be myself, but there are definitely days when faking it seems a lot easier than having to be completely vulnerable in front of people by being 100% real with them. When you live out your real self, you are completely vulnerable because if people don't like you, they don't like YOU—not the person you are pretending to be. It's a scary thing to lay yourself out there like that. People can be pretty brutal sometimes.
—Melanie, Texas, age 17

Most of the time it's hard to root for yourself, because everybody around you is trying to pull you down, and you feel like you don't measure up to them.
—Leslie, Montana, age 14

BEING REAL

When I work on my fictional novels, the one thing I want most is for my characters to be "real." Flat, cardboard characters don't interest anyone . . . not even the author! I strive to write genuine, living, breathing people by trying to understand as much about them as possible.

How about you? Have you ever considered writing a character sketch for yourself? Why don't you give it a try?

As you work on this, write it as if you were writing about a character in a novel. How would you see yourself if you were the author of a fiction story?

4U2 Try:

Physical Characteristics:

Likes:

Dislikes:

Family structure:

Important relationships:

Future dreams and goals:

What is this character's main motivation? What does she want more than anything?

If this character could excel at one thing, what would she choose?

What obstacles does this character face?

What is something lovable about this character?

What should readers/others root for?

So, did you learn anything about yourself by doing this activity? I hope so. I hope you found dozens of wonderful things that you could root for. Whether we like to believe it or not, *we* are our biggest motivator. Our opinion of ourselves makes the difference in all of our actions and reactions.

Maybe you found this a hard activity to do—especially

talking about how wonderful you are! I don't know about you, but I'm more likely to pick myself apart, and find *all* my weaknesses, rather than focus on my strengths and discover things to root for. This is a bad habit, and one that most people struggle with.

Yet one thing that helps me to root for myself is realizing that God *is* the Writer who designed *my* unique character sketch. He designed me, you, all of us—and created us with unique likes and dislikes, strengths and weaknesses . . . for the glory of *His* kingdom.

My favorite Bible verse of all time is Zephaniah 3:17. I love this verse because it reminds me that God made me real (not plastic and fake like the people on TV), and He roots for me, even when I look in the mirror and don't see much to root for.

> The LORD your God is with you,
>   he is mighty to save.
> He will take great delight in you,
>   he will quiet you with his love,
>   he will rejoice over you with singing.

God not only roots for you, He "takes great delight" in you. He said so Himself! When you focus on God, He *will* quiet any anxious and overbearing thoughts. He also rejoices over you with singing. Did you catch that? God sings over YOU!

Now, look over your character sketch once again. Instead of seeing those things through the eyes of a fiction writer . . . view them from the eyes of the *Author of life.*

How does God root for you? What things can He settle your mind about? What things does He want to help you with? Use the space that follows to jot those things down too.

From now on, when you struggle with rooting for yourself, consider God cheering *for you.* You are wonderful. You are delightful in His sight. Just listen to His song.

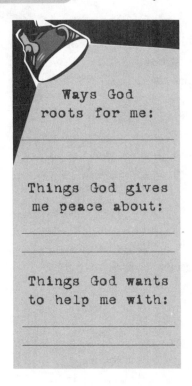

Ways God
roots for me:

_____

_____

Things God gives
me peace about:

_____

_____

Things God wants
to help me with:

_____

_____

 Intermission

Like me, there may be some things in your character sketch you wish weren't there. Maybe they're parts of your character you stumble and bumble with over and over again. Or maybe there are things from your past you wish you could leave behind for good.

The good news is that you don't have to be stuck. You *can* be different. If you accept Jesus as the Lord (the boss) of your life and allow Him to work in you, He can change you from the inside out.

Second Corinthians 5:17 says: "Therefore, if anyone is in Christ, he is a new creation; the old has gone, the new has come!"

Is that cool or what? Read over the following verses, and then take time to look over your character sketch again. If you have accepted Christ, how has your life changed? Also, what changes can you hope for in the future?

Romans 6:6–14

Ephesians 2:1–5

Colossians 2:20

My Script:

Rooting for myself is hard; people say I'm ugly. It hurts a lot!!
—Hannah, Ohio, age 13

I find it hard to root for myself. There are so many people that expect different things of me and I feel like I can't please everyone, and that makes me frustrated.

—Ashley, Pennsylvania,
age 17

This is something I've really been challenged by my accountability partner to work on lately. I'm terrible at rooting for myself. My life revolves around the people in my life that I love. I always put their desires above even my own needs. I also doubt myself a lot, which is basically me telling God that He didn't do a very good job when He made me, which is WRONG!!!!!

—Katy, Ohio, age 17

When I look in the mirror I see a beautiful woman whom God created. Sure, I have some things I don't like about myself, but mainly they have to do with my character. I'm not lying to sound cool or anything. This is how I feel about myself, after a lot of working and breaking done by God.

—Anna, Texas, age 14

4.

On Location

(here or there?)

lo·ca·tion *noun.* a site away from a
studio at which part or all of a movie
is shot.[1]

Once, when I was in Paris, I was riding on a tour bus, and
we drove by the making of a film **on location.** (*Okay, I was
only in Paris once . . . but I like the way that sounds.*)

The "movie location" we drove by was made up of a few
streets that had been blocked off with yellow tape. Cameras
and lights had been set up everywhere. Trailers for the actors,
racks of wardrobe items, and tons of people—directors,
makeup people, and helpers—filled the streets. Seeing all the
money, time, and effort being put into that *one* location made
me appreciate, even more, how much work goes into a
movie.

Location, of course, is the main setting where a movie is
filmed. And a change of location can alter the story. The
characters may remain the same (their inner goals too), but
when their location is moved, the story often transforms to
reflect the change.

For example, what if the location for *The Lord of the
Rings* had been modern-day New York City instead of
Middle Earth? Perhaps Frodo and his friends would face
inner-city gangs instead of orcs and trolls. Now, that would
be interesting.

Thinking about this makes me consider how I change in regard to *my* location (home, school, church, the mall, friends' houses). And though it's sad to say, sometimes I find it's *too easy* to conform to what's around me.

FADE IN:

EXT. CHURCH CAMPGROUND—DAY—ESTABLISHING

TEENS walking out of large meeting room. They are smiling and TALKING. WORSHIP MUSIC flows from the open door.

Walking out the door is TRISH VALLEY, 16. Her friend CALLIE is by her side. Trish links arms with her friend. She walks with a light step and a smile on her face.

> **TRISH**
> I wish I could stay here. I don't want to go back.

> **CALLIE** (sighing)
> I know. I feel so close to God—as if nothing could get between us.

> **TRISH**
> I think I need to change a lot of things when I get home. The movies I watch, the music, and . . .

> **CALLIE**
> And, uh, your relationship, perhaps, with Chase?

TRISH
That too . . .

Trish folds her arms over her chest. She slows her pace, then she turns to her friend with tears running down her cheeks.

CALLIE
Are you okay?

TRISH
Can you pray for me? Can you pray I'll be strong?

CALLIE
Of course.

TRISH
I want to do the right thing, I really do. It's just once I get back to real life, I know how easy it will be to fall back into the same traps. Why can't we just stay here forever? Life would be so much easier if we were only surrounded by Christians who wanted to serve God and do the right things.

FADE OUT

LOCATION, LOCATION, LOCATION

If you've ever been to a youth rally or Bible camp, you may relate to my script. You feel so close to God. You make good decisions—you set goals—to live life differently. Then, when you get home, you discover it's so easy to fall back into what you swore you'd change, give up, or stop doing. Personally, I had some wonderful "spiritual" moments during my teen years. Sadly, they did not last much longer than the bus ride home.

Once I was back home, spending time with my friends often took priority over reading my Bible and praying. And although I loved God, my boyfriend was someone I could spend time with, talk with, and touch.

I could see Chase's love (or what I thought was love), and soon I forgot about God's. It was only after I gave my heart to Jesus, at age seventeen, that I realized my obstacles would follow me from location to location, unless I took time to focus my mind and heart on what never changes—God.

As followers of Christ, even though our body is in one place, our heart, spirit, and soul are at a fixed location. They have another dwelling. One we can't see, but a place that should change our perspective on everything around us.

Hebrews 13:14 (NLT) says, **"For this world is not our home; we are looking forward to our city in heaven, which is yet to come."**

As a follower of God, I need to remember that this world is not my home. It's just a place I'm passing through until I reach my true destination. In fact my favorite pair of jeans says this on the zipper: "Life is a journey, not a destination." It helps me remember that the true destination is reached only *after* we leave this earth.

And no matter what changes around me—where I go or what I do—heaven remains the same. God is still seated at His throne, with Jesus by His side, whether I'm at youth camp, in a high school packed with students, or on vacation at Disney

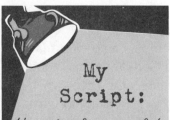

My Script:

It's easiest for me to feel close to God when I'm singing in my Youth Group. With everybody around me just worshiping God and feeling the melody course through my veins, I just feel so much closer to Him than at any other time.
—Leslie, Montana, age 14

I always feel the closest to God at camp. I have time to slow down and think about my life and let God come closer.
—Sarah, Minnesota, age 14

World. He's still God even if I forget about Him while I'm alone with my boyfriend at his parents' house.

It's not that God changes, or heaven changes, it's just that sometimes we forget the eternal—especially when everything around us seems so much more real for the moment.

DATE HIM

Imagine you've found the guy of your dreams. He loves you completely, and you feel the same. The only problem is that although he's made it clear he's available 24/7 to spend time with you, you can't seem to fit him in your schedule. You have good excuses, after all . . . you have school five days a week and then sports and clubs after that. You also work after school to make a few bucks, and then there are the chores that your parents demand. And your friends and siblings. On top of that there is homework, as if you didn't do enough work during the school day. Face it—you're swamped!

You want to make time for your guy, but the longer it is from the time you get together, the easier it is to forget how wonderful he is. And then . . . you get out of the habit of contacting him at all.

If you found the most wonderful, fantastic boyfriend, this wouldn't happen, would it? A boyfriend would demand you talk to him and meet up with him. After all, is it considered "dating" if you don't communicate?

The same is true with Jesus. It's easy to forget how wonderful He is if you don't spend time with Him. Yes, some locations make it easier to touch base with your Lord. For example, church camp and youth services are centered on Him. It's the ordinary days that are harder to deal with. And unlike a boyfriend, Jesus doesn't IM you or leave messages on MySpace to beg for your attention. Yet He *has* written a love letter . . . and it's found within the pages of the Bible.

Have you ever thought of the Bible as a love story? Jesus came to save you from the enemy, and He has prepared a place for your future . . . the perfect location where you can be with Him forever.

So, I suppose it all comes down to two things:

1. Bring God into your location.
2. Don't visit locations where God isn't welcome.

Don't get me wrong. You don't have to carry a huge Bible with you to class, but what about a Scripture verse jotted down on a scrap of paper and tucked in your pocket?

You don't have to stay home and become a hermit, but consciously be aware of the places you visit—does the

My Script:

It is just so hard some days when I get caught up in life and all I am doing, that I don't let God play a big enough part in my life.
—Ashley, Pennsylvania, age 17

Well, I'd like to say that God plays a big part in my life, but that's not true. It seems on Sunday I have great ambitions for the week. I plan to read my Bible and pray every day—do all the things I should. And then Monday hits. School, homework, TV, chores. Whew, I'm wiped out, and I go to bed without thinking about God. The rest of the week goes on the same. When Sunday rolls around again, I sit in church and think, Oh yeah! I was going to get with God this week! It's in my head, but somehow, it never works out.
—Pam, Idaho, age 15

My Script:

I do a quiet time almost everyday including a prayer time and doing a devotional. I also talk to God throughout the day. Some days I definitely struggle. I can tell a huge difference on days I don't do my quiet times. Doing them helps me keep my priorities straight and remember what I need to be living for.
—Melanie, Texas, age 17

Praying always keeps me "on-the-go." When I'm happy, sad, disappointed, afraid, frustrated, He's there.
—Sophia, Texas, age 14

environment bring you closer to God or make it harder for you to serve Him?

In John 14:1–3, Jesus says:

Do not let your hearts be troubled. Trust in God; trust also in me. In my Father's house are many rooms; if it were not so, I would have told you. I am going there to prepare a place for you. And if I go and prepare a place for you, I will come back and take you to be with me that you also may be where I am.

One of the easiest ways to cope on earth (no matter where your location) is to remember Jesus is preparing a place for us. It is a heavenly location promised in His Word, for those who believe in Him.

While there are many cool things to think about heaven, the best part is that we'll be face-to-face with Jesus. I don't know about you, but someday I want to be able to stand before Him and say, "Lord, You were most important to me when I was on earth. I realized that without You nothing else mattered. There were a ton of things I could have made myself busy with. There were places I could have gone where You wouldn't have felt comfortable. There were things I was pressured to do, that I knew would have put distance between us. Instead, I chose You."

When we take time to think about our heavenly location, and meeting up with Jesus there, we'll also be more conscious of our "locations" here on earth—those we should steer clear of and those we should seek out. After all, Jesus is "on location" with us 24/7. And someday we'll be on location with Him for eternity.

Intermission

There are some locations that are a natural part of our life story—home, church, and our Christian friends' homes—to name a few. These, for the most part, are locations where we have space to serve God.

Other locations such as school or work can be harder places to live out our faith. Then, of course, there are locations where we find it easier to follow the ungodly practices of those around us, such as parties that include alcohol and drugs, or places we visit with nonbelieving boyfriends and/or friends. We visit these places in search of entertainment. After all, our society—as a whole—feels they have a right to be entertained and/or amused. We

My Script:

When I face hard times, I write out a verse on my forearm that applies to the particular trial I'm facing. For example, last year when I was so stressed about being in charge of planning prom, I was almost physically sick. I wrote out Phil. 4:4–6 on my arm & every time I saw it, I thought about the promise those verses held for me. I used to write it on a sticky note & put it on a wall or in my locker somewhere I can see it, but I've found that I can't get rid of my arm, so I always see it throughout the day. When I see those verses, I remember that God is going to help me through whatever I am facing.
—Katy, Ohio, age 17

often view the world around us as a stage, and if we aren't entertained, we quickly move on to the next thing.

Yet, according to one online dictionary, there is a slightly different definition of entertainment:

> en·ter·tain·ment *noun.* an activity that is diverting and that holds the attention.[2]

Though it may take practice, one of the best places to fix our attention is on Jesus, on eternity, and on heaven, considering what they mean to us personally. Check out these verses:

> Do not conform any longer to the pattern of this world, but be transformed by the renewing of your mind. Then you will be able to test and approve what God's will is—his good, pleasing and perfect will. (Romans 12:2)

> Set your minds on things above, not on earthly things. For you died, and your life is now hidden with Christ in God. (Colossians 3:2-3)

This may not be the "entertainment" we're used to, but how would our lives change if we just spent one minute of every hour thinking of things above? Can you spare one minute? I know I can.

5.
Hero's Journey
(popularity: getting it, keeping it—for real)

jour·ney *noun.* a distance, course, or
area traveled, or suitable for traveling.[1]

The essence of a "story" is transformation. The process of that transformation is the "Hero's Journey." Think about the movies *Ever After, What a Girl Wants, The Princess Diaries, The Prince and I*—the hero's journey for all of them is moving from a nobody to a somebody. It's finding acceptance, and . . . yes, popularity. Do you think the fact that all these movies (and dozens more I didn't name) have the same theme proves that each of us hungers for the same thing . . . to be accepted, appreciated, adored?

A few months ago I visited Hollywood with my sisters, and together we strolled down the Hollywood Walk of Fame. Each bronze star embedded in the pink and charcoal tile squares salutes the Hollywood greats. There were some names I recognized, such as Arnold Schwarzenegger, Ben Stiller, John Travolta, Mickey Mouse . . . yet there were others (probably radio personalities from long before I was born) that I had no clue about.

As I walked along, I considered the life journeys that each of those stars represented. The star, no doubt, was a shining moment in their lives. Yet here I was walking over it with my muddy shoes, and (for some) just wondering who those people were and what they did to deserve such an honor.

Popularity is fleeting, yet it's a journey all of us embark on. Okay, perhaps you don't want to be one of the "popular crowd," but who doesn't want to be liked, honored, and respected? Who wouldn't want to be considered a star now and then?

FADE IN:

EXT. FRONT DOORS OF HIGH SCHOOL—DAY— ESTABLISHING

In front of the doors a line of cars wait at the curb. In the cars are MOMS with TEEN DAUGHTERS. A few MORE TEEN GIRLS are lounging on the lawn anxiously looking at the front doors of the high school.

Sitting in one of the cars is TRISH VALLEY, 15. Her mom is in the driver's seat. Trish is DRUMMING HER FINGERS on the doorframe, looking anxiously toward the front door of the high school.

> **TRISH**
> Alright, already. What's taking so long? They said they were going to post the results for the cheerleading tryouts ten minutes ago.
>
> **MOM** (sighing)
> Yeah, but they're probably still

counting the ballots. But
don't worry, I'm sure you'll
be picked.

TRISH
You don't know that. All the other
girls are thinner, prettier. . . .

MOM
I think you're very pretty.

TRISH
Of course you do. You're my mom.
You have to.

Trish straightens in her seat as she notices
someone walking to the front door. The PRIN-
CIPAL tapes the results to the door, then he
returns back inside the building.

MOM
Well, are you going to look?

TRISH (anxiously)
Yeah, in a minute.

Trish looks at the faces of the others as
they hurry toward the door. Smiles fill
some faces. Others frown.

MOM
Do you want me to look?

TRISH
No, I'm going. I'm going.

Trish climbs from the car. Before she even has a chance to make her way to the door, her friend CALLIE rushes to her.

>   **CALLIE**
>   All the girls from last year made it again. Katie is a new pick. And . . . there is a tie for the final position.

>   **TRISH**
>   A tie?

>   **CALLIE** (hesitantly)
>   Yeah, it's between you and Kasey. There will be a reelection tomorrow between the two of you.

Trish drops her face in her hands and shakes her head.

>   **TRISH** (mumbling)
>   At least I didn't lose. But then again, I didn't win either. I don't think I can handle the torture of facing this again.

FADE OUT

PICK ME! PICK ME!

Nothing is worse than the conflicted emotions that go along with the above scenario. To feel chosen feels like a million bucks, and anything less stinks. Yet not everyone can be picked 100 percent of the time.

After all, when it comes to high school no one can deny that numerous levels of "popularity" exist. It's as if everyone is keeping score, figuring out where they stand. This all goes on in our minds, of course. We know where we fit . . . or we think we do. Then we hold our breath as it comes down to the honors and elections, or waiting for the announcement of homecoming princess. It is then when the "truth" of who is most popular is displayed for all.

I don't know about you, but for me stepping out on a limb and placing myself out there for everyone to vote on is pure torture. Whether it's class elections, sports, cheerleading, or choir tryouts, it takes guts to give your best and then leave it up to others to decide if you're good enough.

Sometimes the results turn out good. They did in my script above. The next day the whole school revoted, and I was chosen over the other girl for the final spot on the cheerleading squad. I won, and that made me happy. But for every

> **My Script:**
>
> I always have insecurities about myself. I don't like to be in big groups or call people I don't know. Sometimes I don't even want to call people I do know! I don't even like to order food at restaurants. I really have to push myself and keep saying, "You will probably never see them again, Ashley, so it doesn't matter how stupid you may look to them."
> —Ashley, Pennsylvania, age 17
>
> Feeling so different and being self-conscious is probably the most frequent emotion I have—fitting in to one side of the crowd but not the other.
> —Christa, Texas, age 14

My Script:

When I was in middle school, I went to a larger Christian school that had its own little groups just like anywhere else. I desired more than anything to be a part of that group of girls that always had their hair just so & their clothes all spectacular looking. . . . Then one day I ate lunch with them & was disgusted with the way they talked to each other. These people who I thought were the best of the best were ripping each other to shreds with their words. I suddenly wondered what I thought was so spectacular about them.

Since that time, I've basically been a wanderer when it comes to different groups at school. I spend time with every group rather than staying with one. I spend time with the "nerds" because I like to think & have educational conversations. I also spend time with the jocks because I like sports too. Basically, I've done whatever I can to not have any label because otherwise I'll get distracted with who I'm supposed to be & forget my true identity is in God.

—Katy, Ohio, age 17

winner there is a loser. And for every loser there are a half-dozen others who didn't even have the nerve to try.

Yet should our worth really be placed in the hands of our peers? Should those guys and girls we hang out with Monday through Friday, from eight to three, have all the say on our personal value as people?

TRUE IDENTITY

Face it, for any of us who've lived past sixth grade, we've gotten used to people judging us. We get looks over our clothing choices. Get comments about our achievements. Sometimes we try and fail, and we feel judged. Other times we try and succeed, and then worry if we can keep up. We may succeed in one area, yet worry about being a failure in ninety-nine others. We try to find our identity, but it's not a clear-cut thing. Today we feel one way. Tomorrow our mood (and idea of who we are) changes.

It's human nature to protect ourselves, and sometimes that means taking the path of least resistance. We choose to stay in our comfort zone out of fear of failure—so we don't try. We give "just enough" to school and work to get by, then we hope for the best. And, in addition to just getting by, there are always those around us who expect us to figure out not only our identities now but also who we should be in the future. I remember what it was like. . . . (Cue the back-in-time music.) *How am I supposed to know who I want to be for the rest of my life, when I have no idea who I'm supposed to be today?! How am I supposed to transform, and grow, and venture out on a hero's journey, when I can't even remember to turn in my homework on time?* It's a good thing that someone has it figured out—the Person who created you.

Some people were created to have stars on the Hollywood Walk of Fame. Others were created to excel at sports, music, or math. When I was in school, I enjoyed cheerleading, reading, and writing. And now, thankfully, by seeking God and considering His design for me, I'm not only enjoying my career—but I actually get paid to read and write, to praise God, and to cheer people on with my words!

But even better than realizing my God-designed place in this world has been coming to the knowledge of true popularity. Here is a definition:

pop·u·lar·i·ty *noun.* the quality of being widely admired or accepted or sought after.[2]

In high school, I was sort of accepted. I was chosen (after two tries) for the cheerleading squad. I had good friends. I had boyfriends (which is a whole different struggle). But in the grand scheme of things, being popular on earth isn't what it's about. Instead, what matters most is being *chosen* by God. Check out these verses:

I was not appointed by any group or by human authority. My call is from Jesus

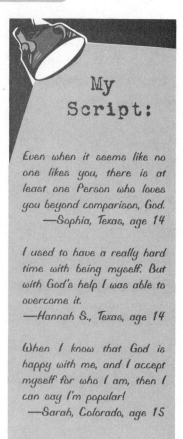

My Script:

Even when it seems like no one likes you, there is at least one Person who loves you beyond comparison, God.
—Sophia, Texas, age 14

I used to have a really hard time with being myself. But with God's help I was able to overcome it.
—Hannah S., Texas, age 14

When I know that God is happy with me, and I accept myself for who I am, then I can say I'm popular!
—Sarah, Colorado, age 15

Christ himself and from God the Father, who raised Jesus from the dead. (Galatians 1:1 NLT)

For it pleased God in his kindness to choose me and call me, even before I was born! (Galatians 1:15 NLT)

We may not be popular here on earth. We may never have a star on the Hollywood Walk of Fame, but we are chosen and appointed by the Creator of the stars.

None of us can expect to be liked or respected or appreciated by everyone here on earth. In fact, if you read the Gospels, Jesus proves that fact. There were many who didn't like Him or agree with Him or believe what He had to say.

Instead, true popularity depends on whom we're popular with. God admires us, accepted us, and sought us. He chose us before Christ was born.

And that is something to cheer about.

Intermission

In most movies with superheroes, you'll find characters with secret identities. Clark Kent hides his strength (and good looks) behind a business shirt, a neck tie, and glasses.

Batman is a millionaire when he's not fighting crime. (Tough secret identity, I know.)

Of course, sometimes we, too, feel as if we're hiding the real us. Sometimes it doesn't seem we can share with anyone who we really are inside. (Superheroes had this problem too.)

In the Bible there is a story of one woman who felt as if no one saw her or understood her, and she was right for the most part. Her name is Hagar, and you can read her story in Genesis 16. Hagar's story reads like a script for the *Old and the Childless . . .* and if you ask me, she got a bad deal. Yet in her loneliest time, she found God, or rather He found her. God showed Himself to Hagar, and she knew Him as never before. Check this out:

> [Hagar] gave this name to the LORD who spoke to her: "You are the God who sees me," for she said, "I have now seen the One who sees me." (Genesis 16:13)

Superman may have x-ray vision, but God sees deeper. Your secret identity isn't so secret with Him. He sees into your heart, your desires, your dreams, your fears. He knows

My Script:

For a long time, I did not want to have a solid relationship with God, my life got crazy, and I just put Him on the outside. In the end it came down to the fact that my parents brought me up with a love for Jesus, and I found it too hard to throw it away.

My advice: consider who Jesus is: He's an amazing guy, and He wants to be your best friend. Look at it this way: If the most popular girl in school asked you to be her friend, you would probably say yes. Well, Jesus is asking to be your friend, and He can do way more for you than the popular girl at school can. Jesus can get you into eternity with Him. Every time I think about that, I can't help but want to get to know Him better.

—Pam, Idaho, age 15

your hurts, your struggles, and He knows who you are before you do. He knows what you need. (Check out Psalm 119 again!)

So, how about you? Do you want to see this God who sees you? The Bible promises that if you seek Him, He will be found. And only through finding Him will you truly *see* too. In the space below write a prayer about seeking Him in your words:

You will seek me and find me when you
seek me with all your heart.
(Jeremiah 29:13)

Ask and it will be given to you; seek and
you will find; knock and the door will be
opened to you. For everyone who asks
receives; he who seeks finds; and to him
who knocks, the door will be opened.
(Matthew 7:7—8)

6.

Decision
(preparing for peer pressure)

de·ci·sion *noun.* the act of or need for making up one's mind.[1]

In every novel or screenplay, there is a character who faces conflict. With each conflict—which can be as minor as answering the phone or as major as trying to outrun a rabid dog—the character must make a decision. Sometimes they make the right decision, sometimes the wrong one.

The fact is, stories are made up of a series of conflicts and decisions. And so are our daily lives.

I have always had a problem with trying to be a people pleaser. When I was a kid this worked great for my parents since I never, *ever* wanted to get in trouble. Yet when I started junior high and high school, my need to please others got me into more bad situations than I care to admit.

In fact, looking back I'd say that most of my bad decisions came from worrying about what other people thought. This affected little things, such as the clothes I wore and the music I listened to. But it also influenced my bigger decisions too. I drank alcohol at parties not because I liked the taste (yuck!) but because everyone else was doing it. I had an abortion at age fifteen mostly because I worried what everyone would think if they found out I was pregnant. Before that, I became intimate with guys because I wanted them to like me. Even more than that, I wanted them to *love*

me. In the end, I was the one who had to live with the consequences of my choices.

Years later the clothes have found their way to Goodwill,
the guys are out of the picture, and I keep in contact with
some of my former friends—but not all. Still, the pain from
bad decisions lingers. The memories are still there.

FADE IN:

INT. HOUSE.
KITCHEN—NIGHT—ESTABLISHING

The kitchen is filled with TEENAGERS
TALKING. A few are sitting around the
table. Bottles of alcohol are before them.
Other teens are watching and LAUGHING.
Sitting at the table is TRISH VALLEY, 16.
Her friends, including ANDREA, are with
her. Her boyfriend, CHASE, is there too.

    CHASE
    Have you ever played quarters?

Chase POURS a drink into a shot glass and
PLACES IT ON THE TABLE before Trish.

    TRISH (hesitantly)
    No.

    ANDREA
    It's easy. All you have to do is
    bounce the quarter on the table.

Andrea BOUNCES the quarter on the table in

front of the glass and it
CLINKS inside the glass.

ANDREA
See, it's easy.
You try it.

TRISH
And what happens
if I make it?

CHASE
Then you win.
You pass the shot
on to the next
person.

TRISH
And if I lose? If
I miss?

ANDREA (smiling)
Then you have to
drink.

Trish straightens in
her chair. She glances
around the room and
notices all eyes on her.
Taking a breath, she
BOUNCES THE QUARTER ON
THE TABLE. It PLINKS
into the glass. LAUGHTER
and CHEERS fill the
room.

My Script:

I am a total worry wart, and I'm
constantly worrying about my
homework, how I look, what the
girls at school think of me, but I
never really think about peer
pressure, or awkward situations I
might be faced with until they
actually happen.
—Jayme, Montana, age 12

In my small school, the peer
pressure isn't really bad, like
drugs or anything, but one
form of peer pressure I feel is
to wear brand-name clothes.
Everywhere I look I see
Abercrombie, Hollister, American
Eagle, Aeropostale. It's like the
people who only wear those
clothes look down on people who
don't. It drives me crazy! I don't
have anything against people
who wear those clothes—I have
friends who do, and that's
fine—but you shouldn't judge
people who don't. I feel that I
will be remembered more for
having creativity and individual-
ity to develop my own personal
style, than I will be remembered
for following the crowd.
—Laura, Michigan, age 13

My Script:

Well, I always try to be myself, but that doesn't happen often. I can find myself thinking throughout the day, Why am I doing this? It's not me!
　　　—Pam, Idaho, age 15

Peer pressure happens when everyone around me is doing or acting a certain way that I really don't agree with, but I don't want to stand out. For example, cursing, or making fun of someone.
　　　—Robbie, Texas, age 14

I guess my biggest struggle is acceptance. I often feel different from everyone else because I guess I'm a "goodie-goodie." Sometimes I just want to be normal and be accepted just like everyone else.
　　　—Melanie, Texas, age 17

CHASE (grinning)
Beginner's luck. I'd like to see that again.

Trish rises from the chair. She motions for one of her friends to take her place.

TRISH (laughing)
No thanks. I think I'll stop while I'm ahead.

FADE OUT

MAKE ME BOLD

Every day we are faced with decisions. Some, like whether to put on white or black socks, have no moral consequences. Others, like whether to drink at a party (or attend a party where there is drinking), do have consequences. Sometimes big ones.

In high school, I made a few good choices, and a few bad ones too. I treated others respectfully (for the most part). I worked at getting good grades. I did drink (I shouldn't have), but I declined alcohol many more times than I accepted it. I never did drugs, but I did struggle with dressing appropriately and getting physically involved with boys.

No one can go through life without struggles, and as you may have already noticed, each of us struggles with different things. Some of your friends may deal with an eating disorder and shoplifting, or lying and a foul mouth, while you have problems in other areas.

It's hard enough making the right decision 100 percent of the time. It's even more difficult when we have others around influencing us. The truth is, it all comes down to who you want to be a slave to . . . seriously.

When you think of the word *slave*, you probably think of Southern plantations and the horrible way people treated others by considering them as possessions. And that is a good comparison. But did you ever think that when you allow another person's opinion to influence *your* decision, you are being a slave to them? Check out this definition:

> **slave** *noun.* a person entirely under the domination of some influence or person.[2]

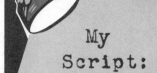

My Script:

The biggest pressure is to find a boyfriend! Golly, what do these people think?! I can't be happy and have a life without a boyfriend?!
—Sarah, Colorado, age 15

I actually don't struggle with peer pressure much anymore. Most of my friends now are awesome Christians, and the only pressure they put on me is to do the right thing.
—Katy, Ohio, age 17

The standards I have are based on things God has shown me. He is the One who tells me what is right and what's wrong. I spend so much time talking to God that when I need Him, I can really just hear Him.
—Mallory, Arizona, age 15

When my friends can't respect me for my decision, I know that they're not really my friends. It's painful, yes, but nothin' heals a wound more than the One who loves.
—Anna, Texas, age 14

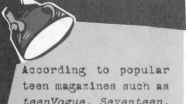

According to popular teen magazines such as *teenVogue*, *Seventeen*, and *Cosmogirl*, the following are some of the issues teens are dealing with. Do you relate? What decisions have you made concerning these lately?

Homework overload:

Fad diets:

Making your ex want you back:

Lying online:

Online love:

When to say, "I love you" to a guy:

Not dressing trashy:

Finding peace:

Having a healthy body image:

Dating rules:

Friendship woes:

Parent problems:

So . . . if I'm influenced by a friend or boyfriend or group of friends . . . and their influence impacts my decisions, then you can say they own me. Own us. We are a slave to those we follow (whether they realize we are following them or not!).

And when it comes down to it, we can either let others influence us most. Or we can let God. This is what the apostle Paul says about that:

> Obviously, I'm not
> trying to be a
> people pleaser!
> No, I am trying to
> please God. If I
> were still trying
> to please people,
> I would not be
> Christ's servant.
> (Galatians 1:10 NLT)

> You were bought at
> a price; do not
> become slaves of
> men. (2 Corinthians
> 7:23)

Conflict will come. Decisions will be made, big or small. Through your decisions, you *will* be a slave to someone. We

all like to think we make our own decisions and we rule ourselves, but look deeper. Ask yourself these questions:

What is behind my decision?

Is my motivation to be liked, appreciated, or accepted?

Who is behind my decision?

Am I concerned about what others would think?

*Are my choices and decisions based on my relationship
with God?*

*Who loves me the most? Do I let those who love me most
have greater influence, or do I worry more about those
who could care less about my heart, spirit, soul, emotions?*

These questions are ones to rethink, consider, and fill in.
After all, your decisions today will affect your journey and
your future tomorrow.

 Intermission

Living life unscripted, like I mentioned before, means just
allowing life to happen without really thinking about what's

coming up next. We know there will be decisions we have to make in life—wouldn't it be better to think them through?

What struggles are you facing *today*? List them below:

What decisions will you have to make *in your future*? They could be things like picking classes next fall, deciding to date, picking friends, or choosing whether or not to attend parties with friends. List whatever comes to mind:

Take time to think about who will influence you the most. Do your friends' opinions most affect your decision? Or your parents' opinion? What about God's opinion?

4U2 Try:

On the next page, you'll find three columns. Pick one of the decisions you listed earlier that you *know* you'll have to make. Above the columns, write the issue you'll be making a decision about.

Now, consider what type of advice you would get from your friends, your parents, or God. Write each one's advice under their heading.

Finally, at the bottom of each column, write that person's *motivation*. (Why would he/she/they make that decision for you?) For example, your friends might push you to wear certain brands of clothing to fit in or match them. And your parents might want you *not* to wear certain brands of clothing because of the cost.

And what about God . . . how do you think He feels about the clothes you wear? Or the boyfriends you pick? Or the parties you attend? If you're not sure, go to His Word, and ask Him to guide you to the answers. Psalm 138:3 says:

> When I called, you answered me; you made me bold and stouthearted.

If you aren't sure of what God's answer would be, seek out a mature Christian, such as a youth worker or your parent, for advice.

There are some decisions that will make a BIG difference in your life and faith. Just think how much better your decision will turn out if you take time to think it through beforehand. When the time of decision comes . . . the work is already done. After that, you just need to follow through, allowing your service to Jesus to rule over being a slave to the opinions of others. After all, scripting your responses makes dealing with the drama 100 percent easier.

DECISION: _____

FRIENDS	PARENT (OR A CARING ADULT)	GOD

7.
Inner Conflict
(insecurity is something we can battle)

con·flict *noun.* opposition between two simultaneous but incompatible feelings.[1]

There are two types of conflict: external and internal. External conflicts are things that happen *to* a person. Internal conflicts are those that happen *inside* a person. One major internal conflict is insecurity.

Everyone faces some level of insecurity. Think of the most successful, positive person you know, and I'm sure they'll tell you there were times in their lives when they weren't sure about themselves or a decision they had to make. Yes, even your mom and dad, your teachers and pastor. Older people, famous people, smart people have simply learned to hide their insecurity well! Or maybe you just haven't asked.

Check out this quote from America Ferrera, star of *Ugly Betty*:

> My high school days were definitely not the best days of my life. I think everything you learn in high school, you have to spend the rest of your life unlearning. A lot of what high school was about for me was not being myself. It was about hiding all the things that made me different and trying to fit

in somewhere. I didn't know who I was. The pretty and popular girls just reminded me that I wasn't pretty and popular, and the nerdy and studious ones reminded me that I wasn't smart enough. I didn't conform in high school, wear all the right clothes, or fit in. But I think the truth is that whatever you're wearing on the outside doesn't change the fact that most people—even beautiful girls—feel the same doubts, fears, and insecurities on the inside.[2]

Personally, I'd rather face external obstacles, such as climbing a mountain or crossing a river, than the struggles deep inside that no one else sees. One of the biggest internal conflicts we have is insecurity. Yes, you know that uptight, tense, overwhelming feeling . . . well, here is how it is defined:

> **in·se·cur·i·ty** *noun.* lack of confidence or assurance; self-doubt.[3]

Have you ever felt that way? Maybe every day? Yeah, me too. In fact it's something all of us face.

GOOD ENOUGH

Our souls are conflicted and we feel insecure when we worry about being "good enough" to handle a challenge that we face. Or when we feel helpless at handling the opinions or reactions from others. Or maybe we feel inadequate to meet our responsibilities of home, school, work, friends, life.

Sometimes fears come out of nowhere. But there are some insecurities that are justified. For example in sixth grade, I was chubby, wore glasses, and had crooked teeth. I developed early, and that didn't help either. I remember the rude comments from "friends." I never forgot the mean names I was called by boys. And even after I grew taller and

My Script:

I feel insecure around guys. It's not even like I'm obsessed with boyfriends or anything; I just don't want to be viewed as a dork by them. It hurts to be mocked by them more than it does by girls.
    —Laura, Michigan, age 13

When I'm in a new place, I'm often insecure. Recently I started attending a new Youth Group. The first time I went, I was so stressed out about what to wear, what to take. Do I go casual or kind of dressed up? Do I bring a Bible or just my purse? I was so insecure because I didn't know these people.
    —Pam, Idaho, age 15

my curves moved to all the right places, I felt apprehensive about my looks. I was never "enough"— thin enough, pretty enough, blemish-free enough.

Two things can happen when we face internal conflict: (1) we shut down, or (2) we seek to be reassured concerning the areas in which we are lacking confidence. And while we appreciate praise from our parents or teachers, and we enjoy compliments from friends, for some reason it's the positive comments and responses from guys that seem to matter most.

FADE IN:

EXT. BACKYARD OF HOUSE— DAY—ESTABLISHING

TWO TEEN GIRLS are sitting on the back porch talking. An older TEEN BOY has a bow and arrows and is SHOOTING toward a hay bale set up against the back fence.

Sitting next to her friend REBECCA is TRISH VALLEY, 14. She is talking to her friend, but her attention is turned to Rebecca's older brother, STEVEN.

REBECCA
Hello? Earth to
Trish. Are you even
listening to me?
Your mind seems to
be somewhere else
. . . or should I
say, on someone
else.

TRISH
Yeah, I can't help
it. Your brother
is so cute.

REBECCA
He's showing off.
He likes you, you
know.

TRISH
No way.

REBECCA
Seriously. He
asked when you
were coming over.
But he's sixteen, you know. . . .

TRISH (smiling)
Yeah, I know.

Rebecca's MOM exits the house. She
approaches the girls.

My Script:

I'm homeschooled so it can be really hard to know how to act and what to do to keep others from thinking I'm just a little freak . . . and still stay within my boundaries.
—Sarah, Colorado, age 15

I feel most insecure when I'm with certain people. There is a way some people look at you that makes you feel about two inches tall & around those people I feel incredibly insecure.
—Katy, Ohio, age 17

REBECCA'S MOM
Did you do the dishes?

REBECCA
Not yet.

REBECCA'S MOM
Can you do it now please? We're having company for dinner.

TRISH
Want me to help?

REBECCA
Nah, I'll be right back.

Rebecca and her mom exit. Steven puts away his bow and walks over.

STEVEN
You look pretty nice today.

TRISH (smiling)
So do you . . . your archery, I mean.

STEVEN
Wanna try?

TRISH
Sure, why not.

Steven shows Trish how to shoot the arrow. He wraps his arms around her. After a few shots, he leads her back to the porch.

STEVEN
That's good. But come here, I want to
show you something.

Steven leads her to the back door, then he
pauses. He wraps his arms around Trish and
pulls her close. Steven kisses her.

STEVEN
Have you ever been kissed before?

TRISH (shyly)
Now I have.

STEVEN
You're very pretty. And you're a good
kisser too.

TRISH
Thanks . . . I, uh, had a good
teacher.

FADE OUT

FILLING THE NEED

Each of us has needs. The need to be loved. The need to be
listened to. The need for friendship. The need to dream, and
grow, and hope.

The problem comes when our needs aren't filled. We sense something is wrong, and we can feel that empty void deep inside us. It is internal conflict at its worse.

Sometimes we look to *things* to fill that hole. Clothes, computers, cell phones. Other times we look to people— friends and guys. Sometimes we just want to know that we're okay, and that we're not going to look stupid or be made fun of. Other times the need is so great, we ignore our conscience and look for ways to get this assurance in any way we can.

Steven was my first boyfriend, and I was blown away that he thought I was beautiful. His attention made my emotions soar.

I realized later that filling my inner need by seeking the approval, appreciation, and attention of a guy led to other conflicting emotions. It also put my convictions to the test. I lied to my parents when he called, telling them I was talking to one of my girlfriends. I disobeyed their house rules, sneaking away to be with him. I ignored that little voice in my head as our kissing soon led to other things.

I didn't realize until later (*years* later!) that inner security can never be met by external forces—such as the praise and approval of parents, teachers, and friends, or from the attention of guys. In fact, it only comes from one place. Listen to Psalm 145:19 (NKJV):

> He will fulfill the desire of those who
> fear Him; He also will hear their cry
> and save them.

Only Jesus can fill our desires. Only He can overcome our insecurities. When we realize who we are in Him . . . well, that is a powerful thing. When we realize how much He loves us, only then can we find peace. Jesus said in John 14: 27:

Peace I leave with you; my peace I give
you. I do not give to you as the world
gives. Do not let your hearts be troubled
and do not be afraid.

Feeling insecure? Turn to Jesus. Feeling overwhelmed? Jesus can give you peace. Do you have internal conflict? Ask Jesus to become more real to you day by day. Tempted to look to others to fill your need? Remember that they are poor substitutes for what your heart cries for. Or rather *who* your heart cries for . . . Jesus.

Of course, these are easy things to say, but you may wonder just how you can do this. I do it through prayer and focusing on God. You can pray anytime. You can ask for peace. You can ask Jesus to make Himself real to your heart. You can ask Jesus to remind you that poor substitutes are exactly that . . . poor.

I often have a three-minute escape to get away with God. If you're interested, here is how it works:

THE THREE-MINUTE ESCAPE

1. Head to a spot in your home where you have a little peace. I like my bed and fuzzy pillow. Or, if it's an emergency, a bathroom stall at school will work!

2. Shut the door. Turn on Christian music if it helps you block out the other noise.

3. If you're at home, crawl under the covers.

4. Close your eyes and take three deep breaths. With each breath, pray a simple prayer, such as, "Jesus, I need You!"

5. Imagine God seated on His throne. Picture His loving gaze. Consider heaven as real as the world around you. In fact, think of it as the "behind the

scenes" part you can't see, with the Director over-seeing it all.

6. Remember God's power and goodness. Thank Him for His love. Thank Him that the reality of heaven is even more than what you can imagine.

7. Offer your worries to Jesus. Tell Him what's bugging you and what has you upset.

8. Feel Jesus's presence as He meets you there. Breathe in His peace.

9. Three minutes later return to life feeling more peaceful and knowing that God is on your side!

My Script:

When I'm insecure, I fiddle with something or try to distract myself. Praying does an astounding job of reassuring me more than anything else though.

—Sophie, Texas, age 14

I remind myself that everyone feels this way, even popular people feel insecure.

—Robbie, Texas, age 14

I see all these people who know exactly what they want, how they want it, and who they are. And because I'm still completely in the dark about that, I feel alone.

—Mallory, Arizona, age 15

Sometimes, I feel like I just don't know what to do. I'm wearing the wrong clothes or I forgot my binder for school, but then I remember I'm human, and no matter what little things I do wrong, like forgetting my homework or having a bad hair day, that's not going to stop me from getting into heaven, because I know Jesus Christ and He forgives.

—Pam, Idaho, age 15

Intermission

So, just what *is* going on in your heart? Sometimes you have no idea. Sometimes I don't either! There are days when I feel sad or happy or angry, and I don't know why. Other days I want to do things I *know* aren't right, yet I have no idea where those feelings are coming from.

It's good to know there is Someone who *does* know. God knows us from the inside out—even better than we know ourselves.

Next time you question just what is going on inside you, here is a good prayer to pray:

```
Search me, O God, and know my heart; try
me, and know my anxieties; and see if
there is any wicked way in me, and lead
me in the way everlasting.
(Psalm 139:23—24 NKJV)
```

There are a few different parts to this prayer:

1. **The searching.** God can look deep inside.

2. **The knowing.** God can know exactly what makes you tick. He also knows what makes you cry, pout, giggle, and cheer.

3. **The trying.** This is the hard part. Because sometimes in order to *show* you what is inside, God will *try* you (which also means "test" you). Have you been tested lately? That may be God showing you areas in your heart that need work.

4. **The wicked stuff.** Yes, it's in there, and we all have it. Some of the wickedness is the sinful nature we're born with. Other things are the bad influences we *allow* into our hearts. Proverbs 4:23 (NKJV) says, "Keep your heart with all diligence, for out of it spring the issues of life."

5. **The leading.** God longs to lead you. But you have to be willing to be led. Is your hand lifted to take God's hand, or are your arms crossed over your chest in rebellion? Are your feet ready to move in the direction God leads, or do you have your heels dug into the dirt, refusing to budge? The choice is up to you.

6. **The everlasting.** Remember, we have many inner conflicts. We have many insecurities. But there is only one Person, Jesus, who can fill them. And only He can lead us to the everlasting.

8.

Wardrobe
(dressing up)

ward·robe *noun.* a stock of clothes or costumes, as of a person or of a theatrical company.[1]

We've all seen the behind-the-scenes clips where the actress sits in a chair and does nothing while the hair and makeup people transform her before your very eyes. Their touch is magic, and soon an average-looking girl becomes a stunning starlet.

Just as important are the wardrobe people. They are the ones who complete the transformation. After all, no matter how good your hair and makeup look, you aren't ready for the ball until you have a gown. You're not ready for the beach without a swimsuit. (Anyone ever have that scary dream?) It's up to the wardrobe manager to provide the attire to match the destination or situation.

Clothes express the person. They give us a hint of what's going on inside his or her mind and heart.

There is also another part of the wardrobe people see when they look at us. Another aspect of ourselves also on display:

That twinkle of joy in your eyes. Or the deep sadness.

The smile on your face. Or the frown.

The playful hop in your step. Or the heavy, troubled slump of your footsteps.

My Wardrobe:

_____
_____
_____
_____
_____
_____

Clothes may be the first thing people notice, but beyond that they see something else. They get a hint of the *real you* through your expressions and your actions.

So what's in your wardrobe? No, I'm not talking about your jeans and hoodies, skirts or sneaks . . . I'm talking about YOU. What are you made up of? (Sugar and spice and everything nice, I'm sure.)

Kindness, gentleness, peace. Pride, selfishness, anger. Or maybe a mix of both? You can dress up, but you can't hide these inner things. What's inside *will* come out.

If I had to do this same activity in high school, I would have hoped I'd picked some of the same good qualities. Yet there were also some inner things I hid from everyone. I *wanted* to be a good, kind, faithful person . . . but that is not always what came through.

FADE IN:

INT. LIVING ROOM OF HOUSE—AFTERNOON— ESTABLISHING

TRISH VALLEY, 15, her boyfriend, CHASE, and Chase's friend TYSON sit in the living room.

Tyson and Trish are watching Chase play VIDEO GAMES. Tyson and Trish glance at each other and smile. BARKING is heard from a back room. Tyson pats Trish's hand, then he nods toward the hall.

> **TYSON**
> We have puppies in my brother's room, wanna see?

> **TRISH** (blushing)
> Sure. I'd love to. Be right back, Chase.

Chase nods and continues playing VIDEO GAMES. Tyson rises and walks down hall. Trish follows. He leads her to a boy's room with puppies BARK-ING. Trish picks one up and holds it close to her. She glances to Tyson. Tyson's eyes are focused on hers. He looks to her lips. Knowing what he wants, Trish steps forward and puckers. They kiss, and Trish opens her eyes to see Chase standing in the doorway, eyes wide and a shocked expression

My Script:

A lot of people have called me "colorful," which I think fits. I also have a nickname . . . CRAZY! I think that I am creative. I love helping friends and giving advice. I also like to know everything, which is not necessarily good.
—Sarah, Colorado, age 15

I'd describe myself as fun, witty, smart, creative, artistic, friendly, gentle, loving, and faithful.
—Laura, Michigan, age 13

I would describe myself as a talented, smart, funny, random, girl who loves God with all her heart.
—Mallory, Arizona, age 15

I'm a wild, outgoing girl with a side of calm. I need to be noticed.
—Sarah, Minnesota, age 14

I am a very happy, laid-back person. I'm extremely friendly, but I'm also unbearably shy when I first meet people, which is probably a result of my lack of confidence.
—Katy, Ohio, age 17

on his face. Trish steps back and returns the puppy to its box. Chase hurries from the room.

> **TRISH** (calling out)
> Chase, wait, it's not what it seems!

> **TYSON**
> I think we're busted.

> **TRISH**
> You think?

Trish hurries after Chase. Chase is putting on his tennis shoes. She sits down by him, but he refuses to look at her.

> **TRISH**
> I'm sorry. I didn't mean it.

> **CHASE**
> Are you kidding? You say, "I didn't mean it," when you step on someone's toe . . . NOT when you kiss someone's best friend.

> **TRISH**
> I didn't kiss him. He kissed me.

> **CHASE**
> Does it matter? It seems you were both pretty involved.

> **TRISH**
> I'm sorry. I don't know what to say.

CHASE
What's gotten over you lately, anyway?

TRISH
I don't know. . . . I have no idea
what's going on. It's not like I want
to do these things.

Chase rises and moves to the door.

CHASE
I don't want to hear it. I'm leaving. I
hope you can find your own ride home.

Chase leaves and SLAMS THE DOOR. Trish's
face drops to her hands. She shakes her
head. Tyson enters the room. She ignores
him, and instead hurries to the phone and
DIALS her mom's number.

TRISH (mumbling)
Stupid, stupid, stupid.

FADE OUT

DID I DO THAT?

Have you ever done something really stupid and then later
thought, *Where did* that *come from?*

my life, unscripted

We all do stupid things. Then later we beat ourselves up for our thoughtless words or actions. We hate the guilt. Hate when we disappoint ourselves and others. We despise the conflict that comes as a result of our mistakes. And so we strive to do better. We make plans to be nicer, or more caring. We make promises that we will be *faithful* . . . but before long we do the same stupid things again.

One thing I appreciate about the Bible is that it's clear that even those closest to God mess up. David loved God, yet he committed adultery with Bathsheba. The disciples loved Jesus, yet they ran when the guards who arrested Jesus showed up. And Paul, who authored over a dozen books of the Bible, had this to say about himself:

> Yes. I'm full of myself—after all, I've spent a long time in sin's prison. What I don't understand about myself is that I decide one way, but then I act another, doing things I absolutely despise. (Romans 7:15 THE MESSAGE)

Paul goes on to say:

> It happens so regularly that it's predictable. The moment I decide to do good, sin is there to trip me up. I truly delight in God's commands, but it's pretty obvious that not all of me joins in that delight. Parts of me covertly rebel, and just when I least expect it, they take charge.
>
> I've tried everything and nothing helps. I'm at the end of my rope. Is there no one who can do anything for me? Isn't that the real question?

> The answer, thank God, is that Jesus
> Christ can and does. (Romans 7:21–25
> THE MESSAGE)

It makes me feel better that even someone as respected as Paul had times when he messed up. Yet Paul also found the answer. He figured out where to find help. And that is Jesus.

The moment we accept Jesus as our Lord, His Spirit comes to live inside us. Imagine it this way: We once had a wardrobe of sinful desires, but then the Holy Spirit takes over our wardrobe. He throws away those old duds and offers something much better . . . a wardrobe that can be witnessed by all. Galatians 5:22–23 says:

> But the fruit of the Spirit is love, joy,
> peace, patience, kindness, goodness, faith-
> fulness, gentleness, and self-control.

This doesn't mean that once we accept Christ into our hearts we will be loving, joyful, faithful, etc., automatically. Instead, we have to give the wardrobe manager the chance to dress us in these things.

It's the same as if you were getting ready to act in a major motion picture. The wardrobe manager shows up with everything you need, but you must allow that person to complete the transformation.

In our daily lives, the problems arise when we try to change ourselves. We think that our effort will pay off. We think willpower will help us act kinder or make better choices. But the truth is, we don't truly change until we change from the inside out.

Gregory A. Boyd, author of *Seeing Is Believing says:*

> Willpower alone cannot make an unloving person into a
> loving person or a depressed person into a joyful person.

My
Script:

I'm a fifteen-year-old girl who does well in school, I try my hardest, and I'm terrified of roller coasters. But that's not the half of me. I'm a girl who loves the ocean breeze, but lives far away from the ocean. I have a love for God that helps me in everyday life. I'm a girl who has lots of friends, and knows all of them personally. I'm a fifteen-year-old girl, who's not afraid to live life, according to God's plans.
—Pam, Idaho, age 15

I try to read my Bible. You can find the most amazing things in there, when you're really in bad shape. God has a strange way of reminding us that He is in control and EVERYTHING He does is with a purpose and certain goal in mind. It's hard to remember sometimes, but it's more than worth it to do so.
—Anna, Texas, age 14

It is not about our *behavior;* it is about our *heart,* our *soul,* or *innermost disposition.* As such, the fruit of the Spirit is not something we can or should strive to produce by our own effort. The fruit of the Spirit is not a goal we can and must seek to attain. Indeed, it is called *fruit of the Spirit* precisely because it is the fruit *of the Spirit* and not the product of our own effort.[2]

Wow, I don't know about you, but these words are very freeing to me. I don't need to "try harder" to act better. I don't need more will-power. Instead, I need to focus more on Jesus. I need to allow the Holy Spirit to work in my life . . . just as I would allow a wardrobe person to make me over.

My effort can only get me so far, but Jesus at work in me can help me to truly change into a beautiful person from the inside out.

 Intermission

SPIRITUAL MAKEOVER

I love makeover shows, and I dream about being sent to New York with a $5,000 VISA in my hand to assist in my transformation. That most likely will never happen. Yet I do work daily on a spiritual makeover. Actually, let me rephrase that . . . (1) I seek God throughout the day, and (2) I submit to God daily in hopes of transformation.

Sometimes the makeover happens when I first wake up and read my Bible. Other times it happens when I read and reread the Scripture sticky note I stuck in my purse. Then there are those times when I'm in the middle of a group of people and my mind is talking to God about my cares or concerns or joys. It is then that I feel His heart connecting with mine, changing me in ways I can't explain.

My Script:

God's Word gives me the strength to get through each day with a smile on my face. I wake up in the morning & pull out the Bible, before I do anything else. The reason for this is because it really does put a smile on my face; no matter how early I have to get up for school, or how stressful the day may be. His Words are like my oxygen; without them, I would have no encouragement to do anything during the day.

—Katy, Ohio, age 17

Remember what 1 Samuel 16:7 (NKJV) says: **"For the LORD does not see as man sees; for man looks at the outward appearance, but the LORD looks at the heart."**

A spiritual makeover means allowing the Spirit of God to dress you. We find an example of this in Judges 6:34 (NKJV), **"The Spirit of the LORD came upon Gideon."**

In the Bible study *Living Beyond Yourself,* Beth Moore describes it this way:

The Hebrew word for *came upon* is *labesh* which means "wrap around, to put on a garment or clothe." The Interlinear Bible reads, "and the Spirit of Jehovah clothed

Gideon with Himself." In that moment, God Himself became both the covering for Gideon's guilt and the armor for Gideon's victory.[3]

So, have you messed up? Been uncaring or unfaithful? When you seek God's forgiveness, He will cover your guilt and make you spotless in His sight.

Do you want to be victorious in living for God? Only God can makeover your heart, and then cover and protect it too. The Spirit of God can also help you be joyful, peaceful, patient, kind, good, faithful, gentle, and have self-control.

So, do you still think you can change your "wardrobe" with willpower and through your own strength? Nah, me neither. But we both know an awesome Wardrobe Designer, now don't we?!

9.

Blockbuster Buddies
(everyone deserves
a supporting cast)

cast list *noun.* a listing, included with a shooting script, of all of the characters in a script.[1]

Every television sitcom and movie has the main "stars." They are the ones who get their image on the front cover of the DVD and have names that everyone recognizes. Yet these stars would be nowhere without a supporting cast. The supporting cast is made up of individual and memorable characters. Some are there to make you laugh. One may be the main character's number one sidekick. Others make the lead actor look good . . . because the supporting cast member messes up so much. In real life each of us has a supporting cast too. This cast is built one relationship at a time.

Consider your friends. How do they fit into your cast? If you're like me, your friends come in layers. (Yes, as Shrek would say, onions *and ogres* have layers too.) You have friends who are on the outer rim. You like them, you get along fine, but they don't know you that well.

Then, as you move through the layers, your friends grow closer and closer to your heart. At the center may be one or two of your closest friends who know everything about you . . . including the things you swore you'd never tell a soul!

My Script:

I feel like I can be myself with my true friends. I know who my friends are, and those who make fun of me, or who are mean to me, well, I don't need to care about what they think anyways. My friends love me, and anyone who doesn't, I really shouldn't care about.
—Mallory, Arizona, age 15

I have had a few friends that really only care about themselves, and they are very difficult to deal with. I have had to quit being friends with all of those people. In the end, I was hurt and so I broke off the friendship. It was hard, but having a "friend" like that just wasn't healthy for me.
—Mallory, Arizona, age 15

My best friend is graduating this year and I'm afraid to be alone in our social life without her. I have followed her lead for about two years now and now others are going to follow my lead, and not leading them right would make me feel so horrible.
—Sarah, Colorado, age 15

The people who are the closest to us are the ones we trust the most. The problem arises when somehow that trust is broken. Or if another conflict arises between you and someone you assumed would be your forever friend.

FADE IN:

INT. KITCHEN OF HOUSE—MORNING—ESTABLISHING

TRISH VALLEY, 16, picks up the phone to call her friend CALLIE. Callie's phone RINGS five times, then she finally answers.

TRISH
Hi. I didn't talk to you yesterday. I was wondering what time you were going to come by this morning. I thought we could go over our vocabulary words when we got to school.

CALLIE (hesitating)
Uh, sorry. I won't be able to give you a ride today. I told Jen I'd give her a ride.

TRISH
Jen? The new girl? But you always
give me a ride.

CALLIE
Well, sorry. I can't today. . . .

TRISH
What am I going to do? The bus left
fifteen minutes ago.

CALLIE
Okay, I'll stop. But you'll have to
sit in the back.

TRISH
The back? Will a person even fit
there? Is there even a seat?

CALLIE
Sorry, I don't know what to say.

TRISH
Fine, I guess I don't have
a choice.

Trish waits outside. Callie arrives in her
small car five minutes later. JEN is in
the passenger's seat. Ignoring her, Trish
squeezes into the back seat. There is
mostly silence on the way to school. When
they arrive, Callie parks the car. The
girls climb out.

TRISH (sarcastically)
Thanks for the ride. Can you give me

one tomorrow? Or should I plan on
taking the bus?

Callie looks to Jen; neither say a word.

    TRISH
    Never mind. I'll plan on the bus.
    Thanks for being so up front with me.

Leaving the two behind her, Trish stomps
away.

FADE OUT

FRIENDSHIP PROBLEMS

Wouldn't life be easier if every one just got along? When my friends and I are doing well, life is sunnier. But when there is conflict—even a misunderstanding—my whole world seems colored in shades of gray.

Sometimes friends hurt each other through their words and actions. Other times they do it through their silence. Sometimes friends grow apart because their likes or interests change. Other times another person comes between them. In my case, my friendship with Callie fizzled the more my romance with Chase heated up. I spent a lot of time with my boyfriend, and less time with her. Soon Callie and I got to the place where we hardly ever talked. It was only natural for her to find a new friend to hang out with. Still, just because I was mostly at fault, it doesn't mean our growing apart hurt any less.

The truth is that females *need* friends. God made us relational. He made us to need other girls to connect with. Not only that, we also want our friends to be friends with each other. We want—need—everyone to be one big happy family. And when they aren't we can literally feel the conflict deep in our gut.

Sure, boys have friends too, but they mostly hang out in a group. They are happy just doing stuff together, and can move between friends with ease.

Girls, on the other hand, have more tight-knit circles. We communicate by phone, IM, and e-mail (lots of e-mail!). We chat during the day. In fact, when we're together, we tend to talk face-to-face in a tight circle. We have intimate discussions and share with each other things that guys would most likely never talk about, such as our hopes, dreams, and fears. This also means that when there is a broken connection in our friendships, we have fewer places to turn. And without someone else to turn to, we turn inward. We hold everything inside. We shut down.

So what is the answer? How do we foster our friendships to the best of our ability?

1. Be a good friend. When it comes to friendships, the best way to have a good friendship is to be a good friend. Treat all friends with the same respect and appreciation that you'd like to receive.

2. Communicate. I'd guess that most friendship problems are caused by lack of communication. If you sense something is wrong with your friend, ask. Also, if you have something you're struggling with, don't be afraid to share.

Yes, your words may make things heated for a while, but it's better to get your feelings out than to hold them in. Once they're out you can deal with them. You can talk them through. You can come to a resolution . . . and come back together better and stronger than before. Or you can mutually decide to go your separate ways without anger.

My Script:

I look to see if a friend is going to be trustworthy. I look for someone who isn't going to make fun of others because they are being who they are. I look to see if they care for others. I look to see if they are going to stick with me in the hard times and help me whenever I need it. I look for a person who is going to give me their shoulder to cry on because I do A LOT of crying!

—Ashley, Pennsylvania, age 17

They have helped me come closer to God. My friends are the "super heroes" in my story. They come to the rescue every time I feel miserable or sour. Their capes flow behind them when they giggle at our inside jokes. But most importantly, they stick with me through thick and thin.

—Sophia, Texas, age 14

3. Expect change. Sure, you did everything together in fifth grade, yet friends grow and change, emotionally and physically. Some friendships will grow apart as people's interests change. Don't take these changes personally. Instead continue to care for your life long friends even as you build bonds with the new people who come into your life.

4. Consider your friends as unique individuals. Some friends might enjoy one-on-one time with you. Other friends might appreciate small gifts—even something as simple as a candy bar—as a sign that you care for them. And don't assume that the communication styles and ways of interaction that you use for one friend will work for all others. People relate differently, yet we benefit from the unique color these people bring into our lives.

5. Treat guy friends differently than girls. According to a recent survey, more than 90 percent of teens are gender-blind and realize it's possible to have good friends of the opposite sex.[2] While being friends with guys is a good thing, realize that your relationship with them will always be different. Guys are not like girls. They do not relate in the same way. They are not comfortable with the same type of intimate conversations . . . and if they are, it is a sign that they may desire more from you than just friendship. When it comes to having guy friends, the most important thing is to have boundaries—with your words, with your physical touch, with your emotions, and with your heart.

6. Remember there is only one perfect friend, Jesus. Jesus understands you better than anyone. He will always be there for you. Not only does He know your heart best, He knows your friends' hearts best too. Turn to Him when you have questions and doubts, concerning not only yourself, but your friends too.

My Script:

They give me advice that no one else could give me. They are around my age, and so the advice they give is different from what I'd get from a parent. They keep me accountable to God, and when I need prayer for either myself or someone I care about they are always there.
—*Mallory, Arizona, age 15*

 Intermission

What does God have to say about your supporting cast? Have you asked Him?

Personally, I've had friends who led me to no good. Then there were others who led me to God. Yes, it is amazing the type of influence a friend can have. God knows that, of course. Just check out these verses (emphasis mine):

A **friend** loves at all times, and a brother is born for adversity. (Proverbs 17:17)

Do not make **friends** with a hot-tempered man, do not associate with one easily angered. (Proverbs 22:24)

Troublemakers start fights; gossips break up **friendships**. (Proverbs 16:28 THE MESSAGE)

Here are four steps to help you take a closer look at *your* friendships:

1. What do those verses say to you about friendship?

2. Now, take a few minutes to consider your own friendships. Are there any you feel God would like you to work on? Are there any He would like you to back out of?

3. One bit of research says that half of girls and 34 percent of guys get advice on the opposite sex from their friends.[3] Are your friends giving you good advice? (Which means it's advice that God would think is good too!)

4. Finally, here are a few more verses to look up, think about, and talk about with a friend!
   - Proverbs 18:19
   - Proverbs 25:11
   - Proverbs 25:13
   - Proverbs 27:9
   - Proverbs 27:17

My Script:

I believe I'm a good friend because I listen to their problems no matter if they're big or small. I'm always ready to give advice when they need it. I don't turn against them and backstab them.

—Miranda, Georgia, age 16

I encourage my friends as much as I can. I try to understand what they are really feeling inside to know how to help them. I attempt to weave God into all I do and say with them. I really cherish my friends as something special, and I will not let them be separated from God for eternity.

—Sophia, Texas, age 14

I found "my dream friend" in many people. But I think my absolute true friend is Jesus Christ. He's the ONLY one who can fit my description perfectly.

—Sophia, Texas, age 14

10.

The Hottie

(need someone to play the boyfriend role?)

> **he·ro** *noun*. 1. a man of distinguished courage or ability, admired for his brave deeds and noble qualities. 2. a person who, in the opinion of others, has heroic qualities or has performed a heroic act and is regarded as a model or ideal. 3. the principal male character in a story, play, film, etc.[1]

In old movies, the main, male character used to be called a hero. Today, he's most likely viewed as a hottie. Yes, there are movies where the hottie does heroic deeds, but he's really just admired for his looks. True heroes are hard to find. True heroes care about something besides themselves. They act on their consideration of others, and that's what makes them a true hero. The hottie factor comes into play in real life too (at least when it comes to high school guys). They may lack true heroic qualities, but that still doesn't keep us from seeking them out or desiring them . . . now does it?

I can't remember ever having a conversation with my parents on whether or not to date. I just did. I had crushes on boys from the fifth grade on, and·as I mentioned before, my looks didn't interest guys at that time. The attraction, to put it mildly, was one-sided.

Later, when the duckling turned into a swan, I had numerous suitors. And because of that, numerous struggles (as you've witnessed from the scripts in this book!).

This chapter isn't going to tell you whether or not I think you should date. I'll take the easy road and leave that between you and your parents. Instead, I'm going to encourage you to take a closer look at your needs, your motivations, and your heart.

So what is in your heart? Self-interest, maybe? (I can't get more blunt than that.) Why do you want a hero (or a hottie)? To have someone to connect with? To feel appreciated? To feel popular? Or maybe just because that's what everyone does—on television, in the movies, and in normal high school life. Me, me, me . . .

In movies we know right away if there is going to be romance. That's because directors know that for the romance to be believable, the attraction between two people must be quickly established. Right from the beginning we have an idea of who will end up with whom. In fact, we're highly disappointed if they *don't* get together at the end. The fun part is watching the ups and downs of true love finally matching up. But we know the ups and downs of real-life matching up is *not* so fun!

When it came to my life, I also wanted to know right away if the attraction was mutual. I wanted to know what the guy thought about me. I wanted him to tell me those thoughts. I wanted to test to see if he thought I was better than all the other girls. I wanted him to choose me.

That sounds a little one-sided, doesn't it? *I wanted, I wanted, I wanted.* Poor me! Poor boys! No wonder those relationships were such a mess.

FADE IN:

**EXT. LAWN IN FRONT
OF HIGH SCHOOL—
AFTERNOON—ESTABLISHING**

TRISH VALLEY, 15, is at cheerleading practice. She and the other DOZEN GIRLS, including her friends CALLIE and SARAH, are practicing CHEERS. They finish a cheer and take a break, drinking from water bottles. They notice the FOOTBALL PLAYERS exiting the football field. Trish's attention turns to one football player in particular.

>   **TRISH**
>   Hey, who is that new guy? The one
>   with the blond hair.

>   **CALLIE** (gushing)
>   Oh yeah, I met him a few days ago.
>   He's so cute. I think his name is
>   Chaz or Cade or something like that.

>   **SARAH**
>   Chase. His name is Chase. His parents
>   just moved to town.

>   **TRISH**
>   Really? What else do you know about
>   him? Does he drive? Have a girl-
>   friend?

>   **CALLIE**
>   Gee, you're a little eager, aren't

you? Didn't you just break up with
someone?

SARAH
And aren't you going to give anyone
else a chance?

Before Trish has a chance to respond, the
coach BLOWS HER WHISTLE. The cheerleaders
pick up their pom-poms and they do another
CHEER. The football players watch them as
they pass. When the cheer is over, Trish
turns toward her friends.

TRISH
Come on, I was just asking. He's new
to town. I'm curious, that's all.

CALLIE
Uh-huh. I've heard that one before. I
think you just like being the first
to snag the new guy.

Trish shrugs. She looks over at him one
more time and waves. Chase waves back.

TRISH
See . . . I'm just being friendly.

FADE OUT

My Script:

I wish I had a boyfriend. To me if you have a boyfriend, you're sort of popular.
—Robbie, Texas, age 14

I have a great boyfriend, and I could not see me without him. But I am pretty independent. I feel that if we hadn't gotten together I would probably just be flying solo, which is okay with me. I don't feel like I have to have a guy attached to my arm every minute of the day.
—Hannah S., Texas, age 14

I think everyone dates mostly because on television and movies you see couples and their drama. Also, all I have to do is walk two steps down any hallway at school, and I'll see couples kissing and holding hands. It makes you want what they have.
—Shelby, Iowa, age 15

BOY + GIRL = ?

Relationships between men and women aren't a bad thing . . . after all, they are designed by God. When God created Adam and Eve, He put them in the garden and declared His work "good." (Of course, they were adults too.) That is before sin entered in. And self-centeredness. Self-centeredness, in fact, is the biggest killer of relationships . . . especially if it is what brings people together in the first place.

Think about it. You want a boyfriend, someone to make you feel special, someone to love you. Someone to spend time with. You have needs, and you're sure there is a perfect guy out there ready to fill them.

A guy comes into a relationship with needs of his own. A need to get respect from other guys for snagging a girl. A need to feel appreciated. A need for physical touch and closeness . . . seriously.

While God made women to get their needs (mostly) filled by connecting emotionally with friends and with a significant other, God made guys to get their needs (mostly) filled by connecting physically. Not that that's what *all* guys are after when you date them . . . but that is how guys *feel* love. It's the way

God made things to work in a marriage relationship. But dating isn't marriage . . . although many people like to play like it is.

I'm being blunt because according to www.teenpregnancy .org, 63 percent of all high school seniors have had sex at least once.[2] That's nearly two out of every three high schoolers! And that is just counting "going all the way." That doesn't even include all the steps that lead up to the big plunge.

You don't have to question why this is; just look at TV and movies. How do people show their love in dramatic features? They jump into bed! Of course, rarely are the consequences shown. After all, consequences aren't glamorous.

Still, I want you to think about consequences by thinking of a funnel.

My Script:

I try really hard not to have it be very important, but it's really hard sometimes when people are always telling you that you would look good with this guy or that dude. Also, it's really nice to have someone that is there for you and that you can talk to. It's not like I'm going to die if I don't have one, but it is nice.
—Sarah, Colorado, age 15

I'm not saying guys only think about sex, but they definitely are not going to be thinking about a wedding. Girls think about long-term relationships; guys think about what is happening right now. Girls are looking for guys who love them; guys are looking for a girl who they can hold and kiss.
—Sarah, Minnesota, age 14

1. Imagine running your finger over the top edge of a funnel. You have a full circle of friendships and choices and relationships to enjoy.

2. But say you decide you want to become involved with someone. I don't mean intimately involved only, but emotionally involved. (Move your finger down, into the funnel.) When you commit yourself to one person, you have less freedom. You have less room to enjoy other relationships.

3. With each step of intimacy you take, you commit yourself more and more to one person, and your freedoms are even more limited. Also, the more intimate you become with one other person, the more consequences you will face—physically, emotionally, spiritually.

4. If you continue on this path and become engaged in a sexual relationship, the consequences can be so restrictive there is no place to move. After all, pregnancy and a sexually transmitted disease will affect you for life. And that's not even counting the emotional attachment and spiritual bond you'll always have with that other person.

   Once you slide down the funnel, there is no climbing back up to the top. Yes, you can repent and be reconciled with Christ. (Look at page 215 for information on doing just this.) Still, you will never have the freedoms you once had. And the memories—as I discovered—aren't quick to fade.

So, in the end, when you seek a relationship with a guy to meet your needs, are your needs really met? Did you get the everlasting love, approval, and emotional bond you desired from a high school romance? Did you find the hero you were looking for? I'll leave that up to you to decide.

Intermission

I was going to use this intermission to chat about two important passages on this subject: Song of Solomon 2:7 and 2 Corinthians 6:14–16. Instead, I read through the questionnaires that were sent in for this book, and I discovered Katy and Hannah already did that!

Read what these two teens had to say, and then look up these verses for yourself. What is God saying to *you* about these Scripture verses? There is space for you to write your thoughts too.

Some things are black & white, like, don't kill. But "don't date" or "do date" isn't in the Bible. The one verse I have found is "Do not awaken or arouse love until it so desires." In my opinion, love doesn't want to be woken up until you're ready to think about marriage. If you can date without getting too attached, not only physically but ALSO emotionally, then go on & date. The thing is, most people do get too involved, even if it's only emotions.

My Script:

A guy can sweet talk a girl with flattering words and at the same time push her into a relationship that she would have rather avoided. She would have found what she wanted, a romance story. And he would have found what he wanted, a toy to play with. But toys only last until you throw them away.

—Sophia, Texas, age 14

Someone once told me, relationships end with breaking up or marriage. At this point in my life, I'm not ready for marriage, so breaking up is the logical end to relationships. I'm not fond of the "date-for-three-weeks" thing either.

Dating in high school isn't bad necessarily, I don't think, but it's not always for the best either. As far as actually NEEDING a boyfriend, I don't. I don't want to need a guy until I meet the one I want to marry. Until then, I'll stick to needing God.

—Katy, Ohio, age 17

My Script:

I think that there is so much pressure because people think that dating and having a boyfriend is the only way to seem more mature. I'm disgusted that kids as young as fifth grade have boyfriends and girlfriends. I think that it's also a way for people to think that you are older than you are. Kids are trying to grow up way too fast because of dating and the stress of having a boyfriend/girlfriend. I don't think that this is what God wants at all!
—Mallory, Arizona, age 15

I had my first real boyfriend when I was 14, and I really just wanted someone that was there for me . . . and that I could laugh and cry with. Someone that didn't want me just because of my body but that liked me for who I am. I think I watch too many fairy tale movies!
—Sarah, Colorado, age 15

See, you don't have sex until you're married because that unites the two people as one. But you can also get too close emotionally. I've personally done this. One of the two serious relationships I had was with this guy who was amazing!! And eventually, it got to the point where it felt like he was the other half of me. Keep in mind that this guy had made a vow not to kiss until his wedding day, so we hadn't gone anywhere physically, but emotionally, I had gone way too far. I allowed him to have my heart & I had his.

We woke up love way before it had finished its beauty sleep. But when you let love sleep until its ready, just like it says in Song of Solomon, it is the most beautiful thing you could imagine. (So I've been told.)

Katy, Ohio, age 17

It definitely makes it easier to date someone that believes the same things you do. Dating a nonbeliever can get really complicated. It could end up taking you away from God. I will have to say that it is wrong because in 2 Corinthians 6:14–16 it says, "Do not be yoked together with unbelievers. For what do righteousness and wickedness have in common? Or what fellowship can light have with darkness?"

Hannah S., Texas, age 14

What are your thoughts? What is God telling you about this?

My Script:

I started dating this year. I was hoping just to have some fun, but as time went on, I noticed that relationships are complicated. You can't just go out with someone and expect to not get hurt when it is over.

—Sarah, Minnesota, age 14

It used to be really important to me because I didn't feel loved. I wanted to feel that love I thought a guy would give me. I mean, after watching any chick flick I would want what they got in the end. But I came to the realization that God's love is the only love I truly need. And if I found love in Him first then I would be able to find love in a guy. And if I didn't get His love I was okay with just God's love because His love fills any holes in a heart!

—Ashley, Pennsylvania, age 17

11.

Admission
(what does beauty cost?)

ad·mis·sion *noun.* the price paid for
entrance, as to a theater or ball park.[1]

It is true that we are the scriptwriters for our lives, but let's
not forget the tons of input streaming into our ears. Or the
images that flash before our eyes daily, hourly, minute by
minute. One of the biggies, of course, is the media.
Personally, I love watching movies and reality TV. I rarely go
a day without listening to music or thumbing through magazines. I consider these things entertainment . . . but are they
more than that?

The messages transmitted 24/7 not only entertain us,
they often influence without us realizing it. I find myself
shopping for brand names I see worn by TV sitcom stars. I fix
my hair like Reece Witherspoon. I apply my eye makeup like
some model I saw in a magazine. These are obvious, but
there are more subtle messages too.

Through media, I often get the hint that I'm not "enough"—
good enough, thin enough, dressed well enough. Or I'm
"too." Too short. Too wide. Too uninteresting. Too untalented.
Too ordinary.

I don't often think of those rich/famous/Hollywood
people as part of my supporting cast, but if I let J-Lo impact
my clothing decisions, then she *is* an influence. It's almost as
if she's in that dressing room with me, pointing out what I

should/shouldn't buy. And just what does all this influence cost?

When most of us think of the word *admission*, we think of the money we pay to get into a movie theater. Yet maybe we should think of the cost of feeling like we belong.

There is a price to pay for admission into acceptance. We spend time, money, and tons of effort to try to be good enough or look our best. The truth is, while all this entertainment and fashion education may help us look good on the outside (and cost a pretty penny while doing it), none of it helps when it comes to making over the soul. And isn't that what matters most?

FADE IN:

INT. TEEN GIRL'S BEDROOM—NIGHT—ESTABLISHING

A group of SIX GIRLS lounge on the bed and floor. MTV is on the television set.

My Script:

I recently got a teen pageant thing in the mail, and it made me think, Oh, I'm too fat or not pretty enough to enter. I also thought, Only girls who look like models enter pageants.

Then, it's like God shouted it out to me. He reminded me, I'm not fat, and I'm attractive. And if I wanted to enter, I could have.

I get teen and fashion magazines in the mail, so I often see what girls think that you have to look like or be like for anyone to accept you. It definitely affects me. Now, I try to not compare myself to the girl who must have Photoshop used on her to make her look the way she is.

—Shelby, Iowa, age 15

Media had a huge effect on my life. I actually participated in a 30-day media fast with my youth group. No TV, movies, magazines, computers, anything for 30 days. The first 3 days were like torture, I never thought I'd make it. But after a while, I saw the good in it. That media fast was almost a year ago, and I still rarely watch TV just because I got so used to not watching it. I also enjoyed not being affected by what Hollywood said was beauty.

—Katy, Ohio, age 17

My Script:

The media used to have a big impact on my life until I saw this video of a pic for a billboard being made. They showed this woman, a normal woman you'd see at the mall, and they were making her up for a billboard pic. After hours of makeup and hair stuff, they changed her face by computer! I mean, really. At the end of the thing, you could hardly tell that the pic and the woman were one and the same! And then they showed you the billboard. We constantly measure ourselves to something that doesn't even exist! The magazines are the same; anything with the media is pretty much the same way.
—Anna, Texas, age 14

I do not want to look like the women I see on television. They look like walking, talking Barbie dolls that are "overly perfect." Real women don't even look like that. I'd rather be like my mom than a pop star any day!
—Sophia, Texas, age 14

Some of the girls are FLIPPING through copies of *Seventeen* magazine. TRISH VALLEY is sitting on the floor painting her toenails.

TRISH
Oh my gosh, I love that hairstyle. Do you think mine would do that?

Trish lifts her hand and starts to BLOW on her nails. CALLIE approaches and lifts Trish's hair, twisting it and pinning it in place.

CALLIE (brightly)
Yeah, I think it will work. It would be so cute for the prom.

JENNA
Do you still want me to see if my mom will take us to San Francisco to shop for our dresses?

TRISH (excitedly)
Yes, of course! I saw the cutest ones in that magazine on page 17.

Jenna FLIPS through the pages.

> **JENNA**
> Oh, this strapless one. Is that the
> one you're talking about? I love it.

> **CALLIE**
> With your hair it will be perfect.
> You'll look just like a movie star.

> **TRISH**
> Do you think Chase will like it?

> **JENNA** (laughing)
> Are you kidding? Him and every other
> guy. Hey . . . in that case, maybe I
> don't want to take you with me.

Trish swats a hand at Jenna and they
LAUGH. Their favorite VIDEO STARTS PLAY-
ING, and all the girls stand up and start
to dance, mimicking the motions of the
dancers in the video.

FADE OUT

TRANSFORMED

Perhaps you, too, have seen one of those videos that show
how television stars and magazine models are "transformed"
for the camera. I guarantee with two hours of hair and makeup,

My Script:

I see girls at school and models and compare myself with them. I try to think how, yeah, they may seem perfect, but they have their flaws. We all do. That is what makes a part of who we are.

—Shelby, Iowa, age 15

Sometimes I find myself judging myself or comparing myself to others. The bad thing is I do it subconsciously. I don't even have to think about it. I am trying to just be myself and not care so much what people think about me. I pray for God to help me love myself for who I am and not worry so much.

—Hannah S., Texas, age 14

the right camera and lighting, perfect clothes, and good photo-editing software (which can take off pounds and wipe out blemishes), anyone can look like a model.

Still it's hard *not* to compare. It's hard not to watch the television shows where girls must choose from a host of guys and wish real life wasn't more like that.

In daily life filled with drama and trauma (even minor ones), it's easy to forget that in the middle scenes of our lives there's something beyond here and now. The thing is, we only have limited resources. There is only so much time, money, focus, and praise to go around. And everything we choose costs something.

The Bible talks about this very thing. I love what 2 Peter 1:3–4 (THE MESSAGE) has to say:

Everything that goes into a life of pleasing God has been miraculously given to us by getting to know, personally and intimately, the One who invited us to God. The best invitation we ever received! We were also given absolutely terrific promises to pass on to you—your tickets to participation in the life of God after you turned your back on a world corrupted by lust.

Is that cool or what? When it comes to the world, admission into society's definition of beauty costs a lot. But when it comes to a life lived to please God, we've been given a free invitation. Jesus paid the cost of fitting in with a holy God by taking our sin upon Himself. All we have to do is accept it and walk through heaven's doors with ticket in hand.

But the best part is that our ticket isn't only good for eternity, it's useful for us now. As a believer, God has invited you to participate in a life designed by Him especially for *you*. When we accept this plan, and accept His son, we are transformed into the beautiful image of Christ.

The Bible tells us that in order to serve God, we must turn our backs on the world (a world corrupted by lust). No, that doesn't mean throwing out every fashion magazine or never watching TV again. Instead, it's taking time to consider these two questions: "Who am I trying to please?" and "What is it costing me?"

Are you more concerned about the people around you or God? Do you focus more time reading advice columns in magazines, or personally and intimately getting to know Christ? Just who are you allowing to write the script for your life?

We must remember that when all is said and done, the movie of your life can end with you and God, together forever. In the final scenes that lead to eternity, 0 percent of what the world considers beautiful or popular will matter. The shoes you wore, or I wore, will make no difference. It's the soul (not the sole) that counts.

And, even before that, the same is true. Through God's promises, you have the ticket you need to live a holy and godly life. Living for God may not get you on the cover of a glossy magazine, but the peace and joy that bloom inside can't be bought at any price. Its beauty is something Maybelline only *wished* it could market.

My
Script:

God is the one in the back of my head saying, "You rock, Sophia! Keep at it! You are mine and I love you." Connecting with Him brings utmost confidence and peace back into reality.
   —Sophia, Texas, age 14

It helps to learn your worth is in God and that He adores you, so it takes some of the pressure off having to be perfect.
   —Miranda, Georgia, age 16

Think of people who are truly beautiful on the inside. In what ways do they seek God? Write your thoughts in the space provided below.

Are they caring, generous, giving, and loving? Now that truly is something to model.

 Intermission

The Bible talks about many women who were beautiful, including Sarah and Esther, but it also notes the beauty that God appreciates above all—inner beauty.

These two passages below may talk about wives specifically, but I feel they apply to all women.

```
Charm can mislead and beauty soon fades.
   The woman to be admired and praised
      is the woman who lives in the Fear-of-God.
```

Give her everything she deserves!
    Festoon her life with praises!
(Proverbs 31:30—31 THE MESSAGE)

Your beauty should not come from outward adornment, such as braided hair and the wearing of gold jewelry and fine clothes. Instead, it should be that of your inner self, the unfading beauty of a gentle and quiet spirit, which is of great worth in God's sight. For this is the way the holy women of the past who put their hope in God used to make themselves beautiful.
(1 Peter 3:3—5)

So how are you doing on a beauty-o-meter? Can those around you see where you focus most of your adornment? Do you need a "fix up" of your heart?

God loves it when we turn to Him for help, especially when it means seeking unfading beauty on the inside. Take a few minutes and write a note to God about the beauty you desire. Beauty that starts in the heart.

My Script:

The only thing that helps me not to compare is to hold on to the promises God gives me about who I am. One of my favorites is that I am fearfully and wonderfully made. I also think about the fact that I am a masterpiece created by God.

I personally love art, and if something I painted suddenly told me I had done terrible & it was ugly, I'd be so angry! For goodness sakes, I made it; you think I'd know what it was supposed to look like! Thinking about that normally makes me feel better.

—Katy, Ohio, age 17

12.

Villains
(the people you love to hate)

vil·lain *noun*. dramatic or fictional character who is typically at odds with the hero.[1]

When I think of the word *villain*, I think of someone like Batman's archenemy, the Joker—who looks mean and is generally bent on evil. He wants to take over the world. He longs to see Batman fall . . . hard, and will stop at nothing to accomplish this.

Most of us do not have villains like this in our lives. Yet in our personal scripts there *are* those people we battle. They could be classmates we don't get along with. Or people who are vocal about their bad opinion of us, and there may even be some who want to make our lives miserable at every opportunity possible. (And that is NOT fun!)

While I've never had someone in my life who was bent on destroying me, I've had plenty of people I didn't get along with. Sometimes our conflict was over a guy. Other times there was a one-time event that led to a broken friendship. There were also moments when I didn't think and talked bad about someone behind his/her back. And, of course, vicious words always make their way back to the person. Just like their mean gossip found me.

FADE IN:

INT. SCHOOL BUS—DAY—ESTABLISHING

The bus is packed with TEENAGERS heading
back from a girls' softball game. There is
TALKING and LAUGHING. They are all wearing
softball uniforms except for TRISH VALLEY,
15, who is seated by herself on a middle
seat. Trish is FLIPPING through the
record-keeping book. She is ignoring the
GIRL seated in front of her and the SECOND
GIRL seated behind her.

>   **ERIKA** (rudely)
>   So I think someone screwed up our
>   stats today.

>   **LISSA**
>   Yeah, there is no way I had four
>   errors. That really messed up my
>   stats.

>   **ERIKA**
>   Looks like she's ignoring us. Or
>   maybe she's just deaf.

Trish turns her head and looks out the
window. Out of the corner of her eye she
sees Erika rubbing her top teeth.

>   **ERIKA**
>   I wouldn't want to talk either if I
>   had ugly buck teeth like that.

     LISSA (sarcastically)
     Yeah, what's up, doc? Just call me
     Bugs Bunny.

The girls burst out laughing. Trish continues looking out the window, pretending she doesn't hear them. She glances at her watch and sighs.

     TRISH (mumbling)
     Great, two more hours of this . . .

Trish pulls out her radio and puts on her headphones. Even though she can't hear them, she can still see the faces they're making. With a sigh, Trish closes her eyes and attempts to ignore them.

FADE OUT

SYMPATHETIC VILLAINS

Dealing with difficult people is tough. It's not like we can ignore them forever. And, it seems, just as one conflict gets fixed, another takes its place.

    What are some of the conflicts you're currently facing? Take a few minutes to write down the situation and the people behind it. Also, describe how this situation makes you feel.

Okay, now, take a deep breath. How do you feel? Personally, it gives me a stomachache whenever I have to deal with (or even think about) conflict. My natural way of coping is to ignore the source and hope it goes away. God's Word has different answers, of course, concerning what we should do. But often that's the last place we look, right? Do you know why?

Maybe because God's way isn't easy. In fact, it goes against everything our natural man wants to do (which includes kicking, screaming, and throwing a hissy fit). If we're mad and upset, loving our neighbor as ourselves is the last thing we want to try. But . . . we have to face facts. God's way works.

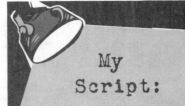

My Script:

The villains in my life are the people who think they are all that, and that the world revolves around them; and the people who think that they can ruin your life and control you.
—Shelby, Iowa, age 15

Right now it's hard just getting through school. You see people everywhere who are doing and saying awful things, and people ridiculing you for what you say and how you dress, and what you do and don't do. It's hard not to just follow the crowd, because the crowd will notice if you don't.
—Laura, Michigan, age 14

My villains are girls that try to steal your boyfriend, and lie.
—Robbie, Texas, age 14

Two girls in my third period class love to pick on me, even if it's as small as the way I sneeze.
—Mallory, Arizona, age 15

Well, the main villain for everyone is Lucifer, aka the Devil. But I'm not sure if there is anyone else I can place under the category "villains" because it sounds kind of harsh.
—Sophia, Texas, age 14

The creator of humans, and human nature, knows what He's talking about . . . go figure!

The truth is, some people are really just villains . . . but they are few and far between. Instead, most people are sympathetic characters. This means if we take time to understand what's behind their actions and motives, it's easier to deal with them. And here are three ways to do that:

1. Prayer. I remember not too long ago when I was mad at someone—*really* mad, because this person was mistreating one of my family members. I was griping to God about this person, and I heard one phrase echo through my thoughts: *Pray for him.*

It wasn't what I wanted to hear, that's for sure. But I did pray. And as I brought him before God, I started caring (even when I didn't want to). I saw all the really tough stuff happening in this guy's life, and I realized how much he needed God. I also realized I wasn't being a very good example of God's love toward him.

Prayer changed my heart, slowly but surely. Through prayer I allowed God to work inside me as only He can. Soon my actions followed. And instead of reflecting this guy's rudeness with nastiness of my own, care and concern poured out of me where it hadn't been before. In fact, Matthew 5:43–47 (THE MESSAGE) talks about this:

> You're familiar with the old written law, "Love your friend," and its unwritten companion, "Hate your enemy." I'm challenging that. I'm telling you to love your enemies. Let them bring out the best in you, not the worst. When someone gives you a hard time, respond with the energies of prayer, for then you are working out of your true selves, your God-created

selves. This is what God does. He gives his best—the sun to warm and the rain to nourish—to everyone, regardless: the good and bad, the nice and nasty. If all you do is love the lovable, do you expect a bonus? Anybody can do that. If you simply say hello to those who greet you, do you expect a medal? Any run-of-the-mill sinner does that.

In a word, what I'm saying is, Grow up. You're kingdom subjects. Now live like it. Live out your God-created identity. Live generously and graciously toward others, the way God lives toward you.

Gee, I had to read that a few times to take it all in. And Jesus is right (of course!). It's easy to love the lovable, but it takes God working in us,

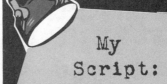

My Script:

When I do run into conflict with people, I do my best to resolve it as soon as possible. If someone is upset with me, it ruins my entire day until I have made it right, especially if I know I'm at fault. If someone else has done something to me, I normally just get over it. Sometimes I say something to them, but normally I just move on. However, if I have done something to hurt someone else, I can't do anything else, think about anything else, or talk about anything else until I make it right.
— Katy, Ohio, age 17

Well, I have a horrible thing called a temper that always seems to catch up with me when I get in a fight. So far, it has been extremely hard for me to control it, so my fights end up as a tangle of sour words mixed with bitterness and hatred.
— Sophia, Texas, age 14

Sometimes getting in the middle of a fight can just make things worse. If the fight involves me, I try to back off, but sometimes my stupid pride gets in the way.
— Anna, Texas, age 14

My Script:

With my family, conflict normally isn't too pretty. With friends I prefer to just wait and see if it passes . . . and if it doesn't then I would call them up and ask what's going on. ALWAYS be the first one to apologize, even if you're not the one at fault. You are more likely to get the results you want if you humble yourself.
—Sarah, Colorado, age 15

and through us, to love those who are far from it!

2. Plan ahead. Continual prayer works well when dealing with someone over time, but sometimes things will hit you unexpectedly—out of nowhere. Sometimes you're caught in the middle of a mess just because you happened to be at the wrong place at the wrong time. Other times you're mistreated because of your faith, ideas, and lifestyle choices as a follower of Christ. I've had to deal with this a time or two, and I've discovered that those who don't love Christ don't care much about His followers either. This shouldn't come as a shock to any of us; in fact, Jesus told us to expect it:

If the world hates you, keep in mind that it hated me first. If you belonged to the world, it would love you as its own. As it is, you do not belong to the world, but I have chosen you out of the world. That is why the world hates you. (John 15:18—19)

When you follow God, your light shines into a dark world, and some people just don't like how your goodness makes them look so bad. It helps to script your responses ahead of time to know what to say. Having a plan takes 99 percent of the work out of dealing with the problem. Here are some Scripture verses to help you figure out how to respond:

A gentle response defuses anger, but
a sharp tongue kindles a temper-fire.
(Proverbs 15:1 THE MESSAGE)

If anyone considers himself religious
and yet does not keep a tight rein on
his tongue, he deceives himself and his
religion is worthless. (James 1:26)

The whole point of what we're urging
is simply love—love uncontaminated by
self-interest and counterfeit faith,
a life open to God. Those who fail to
keep to this point soon wander off into
cul-de-sacs of gossip. (1 Timothy 1:5-6
THE MESSAGE)

3. Listen to God's prodding in your heart. So, what is God telling you about the "villains" in your life? Write it in the space below.

I know, I know, like me you probably didn't want to truly have to love those who mistreat you, but in the end maybe even those "villains" can discover the love of Jesus Christ through your words and actions. . . . Now wouldn't that be something?!

My Script:

I always turn to my friends. I've been working on turning to God first, but it's really difficult because God doesn't always answer audibly or right away. Even though my friends almost always have good advice & are amazing Christians that I look up to, I still need to go to God first.
—Katy, Ohio, age 17

I turn to my mom, a trusted friend, my sister, sometimes my dad. It's different when it's a guy and depends on what you need help with. Some things a guy just can't help with.
—Anna, Texas, age 14

I have a realllllly hard time opening up to people, but when I HAVE to talk to someone I go to my few close friends and sometimes my mom.
—Sarah, Colorado, age 15

I talk to my best friend, Wendy, when I need advice or just someone to listen to me. If not her, then I'll talk to my mom. She's been through teenage years too, and I know she'll always love me.
—Leslie, Montana, age 14

Also, it's important to remember that while most people aren't true villains, there is someone out to destroy us. First Peter 5:8 says,

> Be self-controlled and alert. Your enemy the devil prowls around like a roaring lion looking for someone to devour.

That may sound scary, but read what Peter said just before that in verses 6–7:

> Humble yourselves, therefore, under God's mighty hand, that he may lift you up in due time. Cast all your anxiety on him because he cares for you.

No matter what happens in life—even when it seems like the world is out to get you—remember God cares. Take your worries, concerns, and troubles to Him. God will help you; God will lift you up. Remember, the guy in the white hat always wins in the end. And Jesus considers this battle already won too.

 Intermission

res·o·lu·tion *noun*. the act of resolving or determining upon an action or course of action, method, procedure.[2]

Planning ahead and writing a script of your words can help you handle conflict. And prayer, of course, can change us from the inside out. But there are still times when we all need someone to turn to. Someone who can give us advice, cry with us, or just provide a listening ear.

The important thing is turning to those people who will tell you what you *need* to hear and not only what you *want* to hear. Sure, you'd like someone to rant and rave with you. That may feel great for five minutes, but in the end there is no resolution. Nothing is solved, and your heart may even be heavier than when you first started.

So, if you don't know how to script your responses, or you just need a little advice, seek it out from someone you trust. You may not have all the answers (no one does), but a mature friend, youth leader, or parent can help. They might not have the perfect solution, but they might be able to give you advice on where to look . . . or pray with you until you find an answer. Don't be too shy to give it a try! In fact, take time to make a list of people you can turn to the next time you need advice.

13.
The Critic
(the harshest judge)

crit·ic *noun*. 1. a person who judges, evaluates, or analyzes literary or artistic works, dramatic or musical performances, or the like, esp. for a newspaper or magazine. 2. a person who tends too readily to make captious, trivial, or harsh judgments; faultfinder.[1]

In the film industry, movie critics watch a movie and their job is to rate it. Some use stars. Others use a thumbs-up or thumbs-down.

I do that to myself, all the time. *Do I look okay? Did I say the right thing? Did I spend my time on the right things today?*

I have to admit, my mind never stops. I'm always replaying (like a movie) my thoughts and actions, *and* the actions and words of those around me. I don't take anything at face value, but search out motives. *What made that person do that? How should I respond?* Throughout the day it's as if there's a little person inside my head giving me a thumbs-up or a thumbs-down. Maybe I should call this my inner critic.

The difference is that a movie critic judges a thing. I judge myself. And sometimes I'm way off base. For example, when someone walks in the room with a scowl, I immediately think I did something wrong. When they start laughing in my presence, I think they're laughing at me. When this happens, my inner critic (definition #1 above) becomes my inner critic (definition #2 above).

Do you have an inner critic? What does she often tell you?

FADE IN:

EXT. HIGH SCHOOL—MORNING—ESTABLISHING

TRISH VALLEY, 14, SLAMS the door to her MOM'S car and approaches the front of the high school. Other STUDENTS are arriving for the first day. They are LAUGHING and TALKING. As she's walking, a GUY she remembers from junior high walks beside her.

> **DANIEL** (reserved)
> Well, here we go.

> **TRISH**
> I guess so.

> **DANIEL**
> You look nice.

Trish glances down at her jeans and T-shirt and frowns. Her eyes dart to the girls TALKING all around her. They all look better.

TRISH
Yeah, well, not as good as them.

DANIEL
Sure, yeah, whatever. See
you around.

Trish walks to her locker. She focuses her
eyes on the ground. She is uncertain about
all the eyes of people she doesn't know
looking at her. Her friend CALLIE, 14,
is waiting by her locker.

CALLIE (excitedly)
There you are. I've been looking
everywhere for you.

TRISH (quietly)
Yes, here I am. I feel like
a dweeb.

CALLIE
Really, why?

TRISH
Because we're the low people on
the totem pole. The little guys.
The underclassmen. Everyone else
looks so great, and they actually
know what they're doing. I still
don't have any idea where my first-
period class is.

A GROUP OF GIRLS next to them start
LAUGHING. Trish scowls.

CALLIE
They weren't laughing at you. Don't
worry.

TRISH (sighing)
You don't know that. I'd laugh at me
if I were them. . . .

FADE OUT

CRITICISM FOR THE CRITIC

It doesn't take much to spur my inner critic into action. And
while I'm always trying to figure out the people around me,
sometimes (gasp!) I'm wrong.

Even though I don't like to admit it, always worrying
about others' opinions is self-centered thinking at its highest
point. Sometimes we're so worried about how we are per-
ceived, we don't take time to notice or care for others. If
we're always worried about *us*, how can we truly think
about *them*?

Philippians 2:3–8 talks about this:

Do nothing out of selfish ambition or
vain conceit, but in humility consider
others better than yourselves. Each of
you should look not only to your own
interests, but also to the interests of
others.

Your attitude should be the same as that
    of Christ Jesus:
Who, being in very nature God,
    did not consider equality with God
    something to be grasped,
but made himself nothing,
    taking the very nature of a servant,
    being made in human likeness.
And being found in appearance as a man,
    he humbled himself
    and became obedient to death—
    even death on a cross!

If anyone should have been concerned about what others thought about him, it should have been Jesus. He was God, after all. Yet, instead of trying to make sure He looked good at all times (in looks and actions), Jesus had confidence in whom He was/is—the Son of God. It makes me think I should place more appreciation on my status as God's kid too. Being overly critical of ourselves is also another devil foothold area! One that is also sneaky.

1. Remember Jesus loves me, this I know. When it comes to taming the inner critic, the number one thing to do is remember that we are God's dearly loved children. It also helps to remember that most people are so busy worrying about themselves, they hardly have the time/energy/focus to worry about you. That's not being harsh; it's just the truth.

2. Learn how to receive praise. Sometimes we are harsh on ourselves because we want others to voice their good opinions. For example, I may complain about my hair or outfit so that someone else will chime in about how great I look. It's not the most effective way to get praise . . . but just watch and take notice. It happens around you all the time.

You might even find yourself doing it!

Instead of putting yourself down, start lifting others up. Compliments given usually result in compliments returned . . . and you brighten someone's day in the meantime. Also, if you are given a compliment, remember these two very important words: "Thank you." You don't need to deny their compliment or join in, going on and on about yourself. Instead, you simply need to thank the person for his/her kind words.

3. Be kind. Another important thing to remember is to be kind—to others and *yourself.* What would you tell your friend if she were having the same struggle you're facing? You'd try to be caring and supportive—I know you would.

My Script:

When we don't laugh at ourselves, we tend to take things too personally and criticize ourselves for everything! It helps to laugh at ourselves because we remember that everyone does dumb things at some point and we can learn from our own stupidity.
—Melanie, Texas, age age 17

Laughing at yourself just helps you to loosen up a little. I mean, we all make mistakes (and some of them are really funny later on) so why not laugh? If we are serious all the time, we won't enjoy life and I think God wants us to enjoy it!
—Sophie, Texas, age age 14

Consider yourself your own best friend. Your own number one fan. When those thumbs start turning down, give them reason to flip up. Treat yourself with the kindness and love you give to those you care most about. See yourself as God sees you.

My Script:

I am ALWAYS doing ridiculous things, like falling down the stairs or laughing so hard pop comes out of my nose (which I actually did today in front of the guy I like). I've learned to laugh at myself, because I've realized how funny some of the things I do really are.

For a long time, I was extremely sensitive & when someone laughed at me, I would be hurt for days. But then one day, I slipped on a wet floor, in a skirt, holding a lunch tray & it was in front of basically the entire high school. For half a moment, I wanted to cry & then, I just started laughing & I couldn't stop. I had ravioli all over my new clothes, but it was just so funny. Ever since, I realize how comical I look most of the time & rather than get upset, I laugh along with everyone. That's not to say I TRY to make people laugh or am the class clown; I just accept my mistakes rather than trying to hide them & enjoy the hilarity of the moment.

—Katy, Ohio, age 17

Well, it depends on what I'm being laughed at for. Sometimes, I will laugh too if I think it's funny, and sometimes even if I don't think it's funny I'll laugh to hide it. Then sometimes I just break down and cry. It all depends on the severity, topic, and people.

—Miranda, Georgia, age 16

I recently had a bad day, so I turned all my stress on a younger kid on my bus and was mean. I felt horrible about it afterward.

—Shelby, Iowa, age 15

Even when it's hard, I try to forgive someone who laughs at me or is rude, 'cause I know it's what God would want me to do. But then there are those times that I can't forgive them myself, so I have to ask God to help me.

—Leslie, Montana, age 14

When times are rough I turn to my friends. They are my sister and brothers. If I have no way of contacting a friend, I pull out my guitar and play how I feel.

—Stephanie, Louisiana, age 15

Take time to script how you'll respond to *yourself* the next time your inner critic starts bringing you down.

Also, what things have you done lately that you should get a thumbs-up for? Jot those down too.

 Intermission

The truth is, you're not your only critic. Sometimes others talk about you, put you down, or laugh at you. There are times when we do silly stuff and we know it. Then we laugh along with everyone else. But other times the laughter stings. Our feelings are hurt. Our heart aches.

If that happens to you, here are some things to try:

1. Get some distance. Take a deep breath and get some mental distance. Will this matter a few days from now? Most likely not. Remind yourself it's not the end of the world and walk away. Physical distance helps too.

2. Ask if there is anxiety or stress in another area that is spilling over. Sometimes the other person is going through a tough time and is lashing out. Sometimes you might be going through a tough time and are more sensitive than normal. (This happens to me all the time.)

3. Accept the criticism, good or bad, as someone else's opinion. The words of other people are not always the truth. John 14:6 says,

    > Jesus answered, "I am the way and the truth and the life. No one comes to the Father except through me."

I love this, because Jesus *is* truth. If someone's opinion doesn't agree with Jesus's opinion, it's not true at all!

It's important to honestly consider if another's criticism has any truth behind it. You can ask, "Is there something I'm doing that needs to be changed?" If there isn't any truth to the criticism, simply and prayerfully state your case. And then move on. There is only so much you can do with people's wrong opinion of you.

Now, take a few minutes to think about this. What is something someone said that has bothered you? Write it below.

Are their words truth? What does Jesus have to say about that? Take time to write out their opinion versus Jesus's opinion below.

Their Opinion	Jesus's Opinion

Also take time to script how you will respond the next time you are laughed at for no good reason. It always helps to be prepared and to figure out these things before they happen.

14.
The Mentor
(wisdom when you need it most)

men·tor *noun*. 1. a wise and trusted counselor or teacher. 2. an influential senior sponsor or supporter.[1]

All good movies have a mentor character—someone the main character can turn to when he's lost, confused, or desperate for help.

In *Charlotte's Web*, Charlotte is Wilbur's mentor. She is wise and trusted, and she supports him with her most important, web-spinning skills.

Mentors also help characters remember what is truly important. They share wisdom and values. They encourage the character to do what is right, no matter the cost.

A mentor is not just a fan, cheering you on. And she is more than a coach, who pushes you to excel, training you as you go along. A mentor realizes what is at stake. Most of the time a mentor has gone through similar circumstances and has gained wisdom from a relationship with God. She's a good person to have on your supporting cast.

FADE IN:

INT. ALTERNATIVE HIGH SCHOOL—MORNING— ESTABLISHING

TRISH VALLEY, 17 and pregnant, slumps into a chair at a long table. A few other STU-DENTS sit farther down the table. There are other PREGNANT TEENS seated among the other students. Trish rubs a hand over her large belly. A TEACHER, Mrs. Conners, is seated at the desk.

> **MRS. CONNERS** (caring)
> Trish, I'd like to talk to you.

Trish CLOSES her English book and PUSHES her chair back. She walks to Mrs. Conner's desk and takes the seat next to it. Mrs. Conner leans forward with a smile.

> **MRS. CONNERS**
> You're almost done with your credits. You've done a great job.

> **TRISH**
> Thanks. For a while there I wondered if I would make it.

> **MRS. CONNERS**
> Your hard work paid off. You're on your way to meeting your first goal of finishing high school. It's some-thing your baby will be proud of in the years to come.

Trish rubs her belly. She smiles.

> **TRISH**
> Thanks.

MRS. CONNERS
Also, I was wondering if you thought about graduating?

TRISH
Like getting my diploma?

MRS. CONNERS
Yes, on stage, at the graduation ceremony with your class. Have you thought about that?

Trish glances down at her belly.

TRISH
Yeah, well, I don't think I'd want to go on stage with a basketball under my graduation gown.

MRS. CONNERS
Let's think about this: how long have you gone to school with the same group of kids?

My Script:

At this time, in the teenage years, everything is at stake. My whole future is strongly affected by the choices I make now. This is the time where I decide who my friends will be, what kind of relationships I want, what my values are, what person I want to be. I decide what I'll stay away from and what I'll draw near to. At these times, I decide my identity. For a teenager, that can either make or break you.
—*Laura, Michigan, age 14*

I turn to friends, parents, God. His word (especially James) has great advice on everything, modern or not.
—*Shelby, Iowa, age 15*

I often turn to my best girlfriend. She is really smart and thinks everything out before she does anything. She also believes in God and trusts Him.
—*Hannah S., Texas, age 15*

I turn to books mostly and sometimes friends. There are a lot of good books out there that have great advice in them.
—*Sarah, Colorado, age 15*

Since kindergarten. I've known them
my whole life.

MRS. CONNERS
Do you think they'll give you a hard
time? Tease you?

TRISH
Most likely not to my face.

MRS. CONNERS
And if they did, so what? I think
looking back and knowing you gradu-
ated with your class will mean a lot
more to you than a few chuckles here
or there . . . which, of course,
might not happen at all.

TRISH
Well, I suppose I can think about it.

MRS. CONNERS
You do that, and in the meantime,
I've already asked about a graduation
gown. The school has one you can use,
free of charge.

FADE OUT

WISDOM'S PUSH AND SHOVE

wis·dom *noun*. the ability to discern or judge what is true, right, or lasting; insight.[2]

As shown in the above script, sometimes mentors do more than just give advice. They also nudge characters in the right direction. I've had Sunday school and high school teachers do this. After dropping out of regular high school as a senior, I finished my credits at an alternative high school. The teacher there was *very* encouraging and supportive. She helped me to think about my future and pushed me, ever so gently, in all the right directions, such as graduating on stage (which I did) and applying for college (I did that too).

Mentors remind you not to stay where you are. They don't want you to live on the edge, balancing between right and wrong living. Instead, they'd rather have you come to a spacious place in a solid relationship with Christ. Here is an example of that from Max Lucado:

My Script:

Wisdom, to me, means that you know how to have fun but be responsible, laugh but be serious, and be strict but kind. When you know how to accept failure but keep on going, how to give advice without hurting, how to be a friend, and how to be happy. All this comes from God, no exceptions. There are other things that are wisdom, but these to me are some of the most important.
—Anna, Texas, age 14

Wisdom is a lot more than knowledge. You can be the smartest person in the world, but still not be wise. Wisdom is given by God. It's not only having the head-knowledge, but having the heart-knowledge.
—Leslie, Montana, age 14

Wisdom is not just being smart. It is the ability to evaluate choices and help others evaluate theirs. I find wisdom when I am alone in my room listening to God. I find wisdom when I am talking to my friends, and I find wisdom in the Bible hidden within verses.
—Sarah, Minnesota, age 15

I like the story of the little boy who fell out of bed. When his mom asked him what happened, he answered, "I don't know. I guess I stayed too close to where I got in."

Easy to do the same with our faith. It's tempting just to stay where we got in and never move.

Pick a time in the not-too-distant past. A year or two ago. Now ask yourself a few questions. How does your prayer life today compare with then? How about your giving? Have both the amount and the joy increased? What about your church loyalty? Can you tell you've grown? And Bible study? Are you learning to learn? . . .

Don't make the mistake of the little boy. Don't stay too close to where you got in. It's risky resting on the edge.[3]

My hope is that this book will be a long-distance mentoring relationship between you and me. And as your mentor (got ya!), I'd encourage you to answer Max Lucado's questions:

How does your prayer life today compare with then?

How about your giving—not just your money, but your time? Have both the amount and the joy increased?

What about your church loyalty? Can you tell you've grown?

And Bible study? Are you learning to learn?

Working through questions like these is a great place to start. So is scripting your hopes, dreams, and plans within these pages. But make sure you don't stop there.

In addition to answering the questions in this book, also seek a godly, Christlike mentor to turn to for advice. In addition, make sure all the advice and/or your own thoughts match up with God's Word. While there are a ton of people who have good opinions, wisdom comes from God.

God's wisdom is not only for the here and now but for forever too. And following God's ways in daily life is something you'll *never* regret.

Intermission

You may find some good advice from books . . . at least I hope so! But the best place to look for advice is the Bible. Personally, when I need help I love reading Proverbs. It's a collection of wise sayings.

I also like reading the New Testament's epistles (letters): Romans, 1 and 2 Corinthians, Galatians, Ephesians (and all the way to Revelation). Most

My Script:

The Bible is peace and comfort. No matter what you're going through, you can turn to it and get help. It gives you direction. It helps you determine God's will for your life. It gives you wisdom. It can help you no matter what it is you're going through.
—Miranda, Georgia, age 16

The Bible helps to keep me in line. I love the verse that tells us to love one another the way God loves us. It makes me want to try hard.
—Mallory, Arizona, age 15

Whenever I'm having a bad day . . . whether it's a lot of homework, having to deal with gossiping "friends," or guy problems, I'll go read my Bible and God really comforts me with His Word.
—Leslie, Montana, age 14

of these books of the Bible are actually letters the apostles wrote to new churches they were training. Here are some examples of the type of encouragement these mentors offered to new believers:

> Finally, brothers, whatever is true, whatever is noble, whatever is right, whatever

is pure, whatever is lovely, whatever is
admirable—if anything is excellent or
praiseworthy—think about such things.
(Philippians 4:8)

In light of all this, here's what I want
you to do. While I'm locked up here, a
prisoner for the Master, I want you to get
out there and walk—better yet, run!—on the
road God called you to travel. I don't
want any of you sitting around on your
hands. I don't want anyone strolling off,
down some path that goes nowhere. And mark
that you do this with humility and discipline—not in fits and starts, but steadily,
pouring yourselves out for each other in
acts of love, alert at noticing differ-
ences and quick at mending fences.
(Ephesians 4:1—3 THE MESSAGE)

Don't become partners with those who
reject God. How can you make a partnership out of right and wrong? That's not
partnership; that's war. Is light best
friends with dark? Does Christ go
strolling with the Devil? Do trust and
mistrust hold hands? Who would think of
setting up pagan idols in God's holy
Temple? But that is exactly what we
are, each of us a temple in whom God
lives. God himself put it this way:

"I'll live in them, move into them;
    I'll be their God and they'll be
    my people.

So leave the corruption and compromise;
   leave it for good," says God.
"Don't link up with those who will
   pollute you.
   I want you all for myself.
I'll be a Father to you;
   you'll be sons and daughters to me."
The Word of the Master, God.
(2 Corinthians 6:14-18 THE MESSAGE)

Now isn't that awesome advice and encouragement? And just think, this type of encouragement is available to you 24/7 within the pages of your Bible.

Now it's your turn to try. Turn to the book of James and read one or two chapters. Write down any advice or encouragement that stands out to you in the space below. Also, take time to script how this advice will change your day today, tomorrow, and the next day as you strive to follow it.

15.
Fantasy
(truly out of this world)

fan·ta·sy *noun.* 1. imagination unrestricted by reality. 2. fiction with a large amount of imagination in it. 3. something many people believe that is false.[1]

From the time I was a young girl, I have dreamt about time travel. I loved reading because it transported me to other times and other places. I also imagined what it would be like to visit those places—to travel across the prairie like Laura Ingalls Wilder, or to protect doomed Jews like Corrie ten Boom. I'd also imagine what it would be like to bring historical people to current-day living. What would a pioneer think about being able to cross the United States by plane in a mere four hours? What would Moses think about e-mail, IMing, and text-messaging?

One of the best things about writing scripts is letting your imagination run wild. It's doing the impossible and living beyond what we ever could in real life.

THE HEART BEHIND THE FANTASY

These are wonderful things to fantasize about, but if we were to conduct a poll I bet we'd be amazed at how similar our fantasies are. Which, of course, illustrates how similar the desires of our hearts are.

Look over My Scripts on this page and the next. Do you notice any similarities? There are a few common elements, including (1) a handsome prince, (2) discovering one's worth, (3) making a difference in our world, and (4) experiencing love.

Hmmm . . . isn't that interesting? Especially when you consider the story of the Bible. It's about people being created unique and special, but because of sin they are separated from the One who loves them. Sacrificing everything, a prince comes to our rescue. He desires to be with us, and once we grow in a love relationship with Him, we discover a new and better self than we imagined possible. Is that amazing, or what?!

Everything our soul fantasizes about is found in the gospel. In fact, if you consider every book or movie you love, they all—most likely—will have the same elements in common. It's the God-placed desires of our heart, put into story form. The Bible calls these the secret things of God, and the mystery that all have longed to know. Check out these verses (emphasis mine):

My Script:

My fantasy plot would be something cool and magical, like I had superpowers, such as flying, being invisible, and reading minds. The skills would all come in handy! It would be about how . . . cool my powers are, but with a little trouble mixed in. Or I could work for the government and be like a human lie detector.
—Shelby, Iowa, age 15

My fantasy plot would be in an unknown universe—Fairytale Land. I would be a girl who was taken away from her family when she was young. When she (I) turns 16, she would discover her true identity and seek to help others with her magical gifts that were given to her by God. Okay, kind of childish but that's what I am! A child.
—Sophie, Texas, age 14

My Script:

My plot would be a typical fantasy, a girl who doesn't feel important until a special prince comes along and makes her realize how much she is worth, and then the evil force (struggles in life) comes and tries to stop you from falling in love. But luckily you have a helper on your side (God) who helps you overcome fear. Then you live happily ever after. Well, for a while.

—Sarah, Minnesota, age 14

I would probably be some sort of woodland elf, with a pet dragon. I would be self-sufficient & act like I needed no one. And then one day this prince would come along. He would be strong & handsome, but I would act like I didn't need him. And my dragon wouldn't like him at all. The rest of the plot would have to do with him winning me over (& my dragon) & in the end, I would see how I really did need him.

—Katy, Ohio, age 17

So then, men ought to regard us as servants of Christ and as those entrusted with the **secret things of God.** Now it is required that those who have been given a trust must prove faithful.
(1 Corinthians 4:1–2)

This mystery has been kept in the dark for a long time, but now it's out in the open. God wanted everyone, not just Jews, to know this rich and glorious secret inside and out, regardless of their background, regardless of their religious standing. **The mystery in a nutshell is just this: Christ is in you,** so therefore you can look forward to sharing in God's glory. It's that simple. That is the substance of our Message.
(Colossians 1:26–27 THE MESSAGE, emphasis mine)

My purpose is that they may be encour-
aged in heart and united in love, so
that they may have the full riches of
complete understanding, in order that
they may know **the mystery of God,
namely, Christ,** in whom are hidden all
the treasures of wisdom and knowledge.
(Colossians 2:2—3, emphasis mine)

So what is the mystery that our souls have been aching for since the creation of the world? The last two Scripture passages tell us . . . it is Christ in us. It's the love we've waited for. It's the completeness that our souls long for, found in Him.

FADE IN:

**INT. TEEN GIRL'S
BEDROOM—NOON—ESTABLISHING**

TRISH VALLEY, 17 and pregnant, lies in
bed. A soap opera is playing on the TELE-
VISION. Trish watches it for a while, then
she CLICKS it off. She rolls to her side
and wraps her arms around her stomach.
Soon she starts to cry.

> **TRISH** (crying)
> Oh, God, I've really screwed up my
> life this time. Look at me. I'm sev-
> enteen years old, and I'm pregnant. I
> sleep until noon and spend most of my
> day watching soaps. I've made a mess
> of everything. If You can do anything
> with my life, please do.

Trish cries a little longer, and soon she pushes off the covers. She reaches to her nightstand and pulls her Bible to her chest. Then, with brow furrowed, she opens it and begins to read. After a while, a soft smile fills her face.

> **TRISH**
> For God so loved the world that he gave his one and only Son, that whoever believes in him shall not perish but have eternal life. (John 3:16)

FADE OUT

REAL-LIFE SUPERHERO

su·per·he·ro *noun.* a figure, especially in a comic strip or cartoon, endowed with superhuman powers and usually portrayed as fighting evil or crime.[2]

The script above is a very short script, but who said a long dialogue is needed to completely change your life? The prayer I wrote above is as close to what really happened as I remember. I'll never forget the despair of being seventeen, pregnant, and dumped by my boyfriend. I remember staying up late every night watching romantic comedies and wishing I could find true love. I remember watching soap operas and growing sick and tired of the drama. My life had enough drama of its own, thank you very much!

It's not like everything transformed overnight, but from the moment I dedicated my life to God I experienced a change inside. I felt peace, and I felt hope—something I hadn't known for a great while.

Fantasies get a lot of thought, but sometimes I need to take time to think more about the amazing and real superhero in my life. More powerful than Superman, more wonderful than any Prince Charming, at my lowest point Jesus came to my rescue. Not only was I saved from sin, I was captured by grace. And because of the transformation from the inside out, I will forever follow Him.

The problem happens, though, when we forget. We forget about our Prince and all He's done for us. We forget that we will never be satisfied until we find satisfaction in Him. We forget that no human relationship will ever fulfill

My Script:

Some people get so caught up in their daydreams that they forget how good life really is to them and what the real reason we were put on this earth for. Some people never seem to be happy with what they have right then and are always asking for more instead of being content.
—Hannah, Texas, age 15

I don't think that having all my fantasies come true would be good because life might be too perfect for me. If my life were too perfect, I wouldn't have trials to make me stronger, and I might not go to God as often as I should if I had everything I wanted. I might become spoiled and not seek God like I should.
—Melanie, Texas, age 17

Some things are just supposed to be in your dreams. If my dreams came true, then life would be too perfect, and it would make me further away from God.
—Lauren, Pennsylvania, age 14

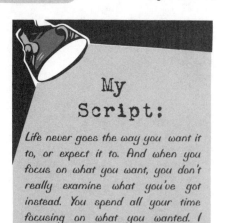

My Script:

Life never goes the way you want it to, or expect it to. And when you focus on what you want, you don't really examine what you've got instead. You spend all your time focusing on what you wanted. I realized though that what God gives me instead is ALWAYS better than anything I could have possibly dreamed of.

—Katy, Ohio, age 17

every aspect our soul desires. And this is yet another problem. . . . We all have fantasies, but if we daydream about ways they can be completely fulfilled by anything or anyone other than God, we will miss the mark. And instead, we'll be discontent and dissatisfied by everything and everyone.

OUR NEED

Like the wise girls in the My Scripts mentioned, if your daydreams are fulfilled by things on earth, then you will have no need for God.

No matter how much I long for it, things will never be perfect here on earth. And you know what? I'm okay with that. Because when things aren't perfect, I start looking toward God, and I place my trust and hope in Him—hope for future perfection in His presence.

Think about it. What things do YOU wish were perfect? Your body? Your relationships? Your grades? When they aren't perfect, do you find yourself turning to God more and more? If so, how does God help you? If not, then how could turning to God make a difference? Answer in the space below:

Fantasies draw us in because they promise a happy ending. I've found mine in Christ. How about you? Think about your own daydreams. How do they point to the inner desires of your heart?

Intermission

Unlike fantasy plots with pet dragons and special powers, we also daydream about things that *could* happen one day. Daydreams are often hopes for tomorrow that just haven't happened yet.

There are two sides to daydreams: (1) daydreams that help us hope, plan, and prepare for the future, or (2) daydreams that help us escape reality. This second type also can make us dissatisfied with life.

Rather than escaping reality, I think we need to embrace it. We need to really believe everything our faith claims to be true.

Sometimes we live like Jesus is a fantasy. We think it's a good idea to believe in a loving, saving God, but for the most part we do what we have to do to take care of ourselves.

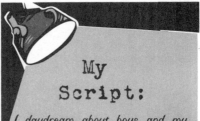

My Script:

I daydream about boys and my plans for life, what would happen if I could do whatever I wanted and get whatever I wanted. I dream about what I could do if time would go back on my command. Usually to stop me from making a fool of myself.
—Sarah, Minnesota, age 14

Sometimes daydreams do make you dissatisfied with real life, because you dream up this way that life could be. Sometimes it doesn't though because it's like daydreaming gives you this "outlet" so you can relax and then better deal with real life.
—Miranda, Georgia, age 16

In our sweet little daydreams, life is perfect. In real life, there are tons of things that go wrong!! I think that when we dream of the perfect life and grow up to find that nothing is perfect, it leaves us a little disappointed.
—Melanie, Texas, age 17

Do you ever find yourself doing this?

Think about your day-to-day living. Do you live as if Jesus and everything in the Bible were a reality? If not, how would your days change if you did?

Finally, script your plan for living out the reality of Jesus in you. Allow yourself to daydream about what a day would be like if you truly lived it out. Now script it happening like that TOMORROW:

16.
The Action and Adventure Movie
(search for the treasure)

ad·ven·ture *noun.* a bold or exciting undertaking or experience.[1]

The **adventure film** is a film genre which has been a popular one in the history of cinema. Although the genre is not clearly defined, adventure films are usually set in the past or sometimes in a fantasy world, and often involve swordfighting or swashbuckling.[2]

I loved the movie *National Treasure*, mainly because I'm thrilled by the idea of unimaginable treasure hidden where we least expect it. It reminds me of a news story I just read. It seems a rare 184-year-old copy of the Declaration of Independence was found in a thrift store. The bargain hunter purchased it for $2.48, and experts believe it's worth 100,000 times that much.[3] Now that's a treasure I'd like to find! Could you imagine?

Like in the case of the treasure seekers in *National Treasure*, or the bargain hunter in the thrift store, true treasure rarely just comes to you unexpectedly. It's something that needs to be sought out. Can you imagine an action/adventure movie in which a rare possession just drops out of the sky and that's the end of that?

The truth is, on a daily basis, all of us seek something. We may not put on an Indiana Jones hat and head off to Peru, but we do seek out things we consider to be treasure every day of our lives.

FADE IN:

INT. LIVING ROOM OF HOUSE—MORNING—ESTABLISHING

TRISH VALLEY, 17 and pregnant, is getting ready for her graduation ceremony. Her hair is fixed, and she's wearing a nice dress. Her graduation gown is pressed and spread out on the couch. She glances at her watch, and then the DOORBELL RINGS. Surprised, she OPENS THE DOOR to find STEVEN, 19. A look of surprise flashes across Trish's face. Without a word she welcomes Steven inside.

> **TRISH** (shocked)
> What are you doing here? I haven't seen you in years.

> **STEVEN**
> I heard you were graduating, and I thought I'd drive up here to see you.

Trish rubs her large, pregnant stomach.

> **TRISH**
> So, did you hear about this too?

STEVEN
Yeah, I heard your boyfriend is out of the picture. That's another reason I thought I'd stop by. You're not leaving for the graduation ceremony yet, are you?

TRISH
No, I still have an hour before we have to leave. I suppose I'm a little early. Come inside. My mom went to the store to get some things.

My Script:

I try to seek out things that matter in life such as a relationship with God, and making a difference in other people's lives. But there are definitely days when I seek things for my own gratification too.
—Melanie, Texas, age 17

I often seek feelings of importance. I seek a need to be noticed and for people to see the real me. I seek this in my everyday life, and most of the time I find it.
—Sarah, Minnesota, age 14

I'm looking for the perfect person to date, and I'm looking for inner peace. I want to live a better life and be more real with God and people, but it is a challenge.
—Shelby, Iowa, age 15

They sit on the couch and share memories about the time they dated and the years that had passed since then. Soon they are laughing and smiling.

STEVEN
I know this may seem out of the blue, but I haven't stopped loving you, even after all these years. I

think it's a shame for your baby not
to have a dad around too. I'd like to
see if we can work things out . . .
try again.

Trish rubs her belly. She smiles.

> **TRISH**
> This is sort of sudden. But I have
> to admit that being with you feels
> like two years haven't passed
> at all.

> **STEVEN**
> I'll only be able to stay for half
> of the graduation ceremony. I still
> have an hour drive, and then I have
> to work tonight. But can I call you
> later this week?

> **TRISH**
> Yeah, sure, of course.

Trish glances down at her belly.

> **TRISH**
> Are you sure you're still interested
> in me? In us? I mean, this is a huge
> responsibility.

> **STEVEN**
> I care about you . . . and I just
> had to tell you. It's not like I
> haven't dated since we've been apart
> either. I still care. I came all

the way up here to see you again,
didn't I?

TRISH
Yeah, that was very sweet.

Steven leans over and gives her a soft
KISS. Then he stands.

STEVEN
Well, I suppose I'll see you at the
high school. Or, if I don't see you
there, we'll talk.

TRISH
Sure, talk later.

Trish watches Steven drive away, and then
she waits for her MOM. She tells her the
whole story as they drive to the graduation ceremony. Trish has a light step as
she walks into the room to get ready. The
other GRADUATES are TALKING and LAUGHING
as they put on their gowns and caps. Trish
sees her friend CALLIE.

TRISH
You'll never believe who came to see
me today.

CALLIE
Who?

TRISH
Steven.

CALLIE
Oh my gosh. I heard he was in town.
What did he think of you being
pregnant? Does he know that you and
Chase aren't still together?

TRISH (excitedly)
Yeah, he knew. He said he's going
to call me. He said that he wants
to see me again, and that my baby
should have a dad. . . .

CALLIE (interrupting)
He said that?

TRISH
Yeah, why?

Callie looks nervous. She takes Trish's
hands in hers.

CALLIE
Well, you know my mom is best
friends with his mom, right? I've
known something for a while . . .
I just didn't want to tell you.

TRISH
What?

CALLIE
Steven is engaged. I heard him tell
my mom himself, just the other day.
He's been dating this same girl for
over a year.

Trish feels heat rising to her face. She grabs the back of the nearest chair, and then she sits down.

CALLIE
I'm sorry. I should have waited to tell you. I just don't want you to get hurt again, that's all. It sounds like Steven is playing some type of game.

Trish attempts a smile, and then she re-adjusts her gown.

TRISH
I feel like such a fool. I should have known.

CALLIE
Are you kidding? There's no way you could have known. Forget about him. Don't get mixed up in that mess. You deserve better than that.

Trish shrugs, then she wipes away the tears filling her eyes.

TRISH (somberly)
I know the type of relationship Steven and I used to have. I also know it's not one God would want for me anyway. I suppose I just got wrapped up in those old emotions again. It was nice to hope that a guy could still love me. It was nice

to be excited even if just for a few
minutes.

CALLIE
Of course there will be a guy who
will still love you. You just have to
make sure he's the right one God has
for you . . . and not just someone
to fill that hole in your heart.

TRISH
You're right. When did you get so
wise?

Callie places her graduation cap on her
head and smiles.

CALLIE
I'm a high school graduate, remember?
It comes with the diploma. Now, we
better hurry. The ceremony is about
to start.

FADE OUT

FILLING THE HOLES IN OUR HEART

Now, that was a sad script, wasn't it? As you may have experienced, nothing is worse than getting your hopes up only to
have them dashed to the ground.

My heart doubly ached after discovering Steven's engagement. Why? Because I had been rejected by my baby's father. And then, when I had hopes for another relationship, I realized that hope was in vain.

You may read the above script and question how one visit, which lasted less than an hour, could bring so much hope. The main reason was the vacancy in my heart. Rejection always does that. It leaves a hole that must be filled. I was ready to fill the hole with the first person who showed interest in me. Thankfully, God had other ideas.

The things we seek out—whether it is relationships, things, beauty, approval—are evidence of what we feel we're missing in our hearts. My heart longed for the love of a man. It was the treasure I sought. But God knew better than I did. He knew the emotional ride I sought was like candy-store trinkets compared to the true riches He had in store for me.

After graduation I started seeking God with my whole heart. I had my son three weeks after the ceremony, and not long after God brought another guy in my life. An awesome Christian guy who turned out to be an amazing husband and father. He is a treasure, for sure . . . but the true treasure that carries me through every day is my relationship with Jesus Christ.

How about you? Has rejection left a hole in your heart?

We may think and plan and dream about seeking out God's best, but in the end we may look to far less to fill our empty places. What have you sought lately? Have you found what your heart desires? Where can true treasure be found?

TRUE TREASURE

> **treas·ure** *noun*. 1. accumulated or stored
> wealth in the form of money, jewels, or
> other valuables. 2. valuable or precious
> possessions of any kind. 3. one consid-
> ered especially precious or valuable.[4]

Just a few months before my graduation, I dedicated my life to
God. From the moment I confessed with my lips that Jesus is
Lord, I knew my soul was secure in Christ. I had hoped that
God would design a good future for me. I had hope in eternity.

I had found the greatest treasure possible. This treasure,
and our gift-giving God, is described beautifully in Ephesians
1:6 (THE MESSAGE):

> How blessed is God! And what a blessing
> he is! He's the Father of our Master,
> Jesus Christ, and takes us to the high
> places of blessing in him. Long before he
> laid down earth's foundations, he had us
> in mind, had settled on us as the focus
> of his love, to be made whole and holy
> by his love. Long, long ago he decided to
> adopt us into his family through Jesus
> Christ. (What pleasure he took in plan-
> ning this!) He wanted us to enter into
> the celebration of his lavish gift-giving
> by the hand of his beloved Son.

A problem arises, though, when we accept the future
riches of heaven without understanding the day-to-day riches
we can find in Christ. The blessings of Jesus are available to
us every day, but we can't just wait for God to plop them
down on our laps. Instead, we need to seek them out.

So do not worry, saying, "What shall we
eat?" or "What shall we drink?" or "What
shall we wear?" For the pagans run after
all these things, and your heavenly
Father knows that you need them. But
seek first his kingdom and his righteousness, and all these things will be
given to you as well. (Matthew 6:31–33)

We can have the promise of being with Christ for eternity, but each day we also need to fill ourselves up with God.
We need to seek out the treasure He offers us for daily living. Otherwise we'll find ourselves wanting to fill our souls'
holes in other ways.

The only way to find true treasure is to connect with Jesus.
Not just talking about Him, learning about Him, and listening
to songs about Him, but truly connecting with Him—allowing
His Spirit to touch yours. Psalm 16:11 (AMP) says:

You will show me the path of life; in Your
presence is fullness of joy, at Your right
hand there are pleasures forevermore.

Everything we want, desire, seek, and need—from deep
in our hearts—can be found *in* Jesus. Ryan Dobson puts it
this way:

Have you ever tasted true purity? That thing called holiness? Once you do, once you come close to the flame of
God's presence and sense His perfection and His love,
you'll want more and more. You'll want to live in that
light, to bask in its warmth, to build a house right beside
it. You'll want to get as close to that kind of purity as you
can get. Because it's better than any of the darkness that
this world offers.

My Script:

I think the ultimate adventure is just being all you can be for God. Others may say it's being a pastor or a missionary, but I say every Christian lives out the ultimate adventure once in their lives.

The steps I need to take in order to be ready for God are really simple and yet still hard. They are: 1. Reading your Bible so that you can know the instructions God has sent to you. 2. Talking to God before doing anything, and 3. Showing people God's love everywhere you go no matter what you do. When you do these things you will live the ultimate adventure.

—Sarah, Minnesota, age 14

If you live the Christian life, you'll have a relationship with the God of the universe. Know Jesus is the greatest treasure you could ever discover in this life. He is the only one who will never leave you, no matter what you've done or where you go. He is your heart's true home.[5]

Have you found that to be true? Can you truly say that knowing Jesus is the greatest treasure you could ever discover?

If you truly believe this, how should this belief affect how you live moment by moment? Imagine that tomorrow when you wake up, you will live as an adventurer in search of focusing on Jesus, in the midst of your everyday life. What would you do? What would you seek out? Who would you ask to join you on your adventure? Script your answer.

Intermission

In every adventure movie the main character faces obstacles, difficult paths, hidden threats, and close calls. Sometimes I wish living the Christian life was easier than that, but too often we face the same things!

Usually, when a main character of a movie sets out, he gathers up all the necessary tools he expects to need. Thankfully, we don't have to figure out want we need, God has already told us. And not only has He told us, He's provided it all! Check out Ephesians 6:10–18. It says:

> Finally, be strong in the Lord and in his mighty power. Put on the full armor of God so that you can take your stand against the devil's schemes. For our struggle is not against flesh and blood, but against the rulers, against the authorities, against

My Script:

When I feel I'm in over my head, I stop, pray to God, wait for His answer, and then obey. It can be that He's putting you through this to prepare you for other things ahead. So if we take the time to ask Him, and then the time to wait for an answer, most of the time we find the right path.
—Anna, Texas, age 14

I look toward God when I feel the adventure is too hard. Sometimes I can't hear Him when He responds, but I always somehow find a way out of a problem when I ask God for help. He picks me up off the ground when I stumble.
—Sarah, Minnesota, age 14

I always get myself in over my head . . . and I always end up back at God, seeking Him. I have to remind myself to trust God and remember that He has a plan, and I don't need to go off on my own looking for a better story.
—Melanie, Texas, age 17

the powers of this dark world and against the spiritual forces of evil in the heavenly realms. Therefore put on the full armor of God, so that when the day of evil comes, you may be able to stand your ground, and after you have done everything, to stand. Stand firm then, with the belt of truth buckled around your waist, with the breastplate of righteousness in place, and with your feet fitted with the readiness that comes from the gospel of peace. In addition to all this, take up the shield of faith, with which you can extinguish all the flaming arrows of the evil one. Take the helmet of salvation and the sword of the Spirit, which is the word of God. And pray in the Spirit on all occasions with all kinds of prayers and requests. With this in mind, be alert and always keep on praying for all the saints.

So, what do you think? Do you take advantage of all these "tools" that God has given you? If not, how could you better take advantage of them? How will it change your life when you do?

17.
The Family Film
(wholesome entertainment
. . . or not!)

A **family film** is a film genre that, like a children's film, is suitable for young children, but with the difference that a family film has been carefully written, directed, cast and acted so it will appeal to all members of a typical family.[1]

It seems like every family film has some type of parent and/or family problems. Maybe it is parents who don't understand or that pesky kid brother who always is in the way and/or causing trouble. (I had both.) We watch these family comedies and laugh. We nod our head in understanding, because our crazy homes are similar in so many ways.

Family relationships are some of the hardest ones to deal with. Why? Well, the old saying is true: "You can pick your friends, but you're stuck with your family members." People with all different personality types are related—personalities we'd never choose to interact with if they weren't our flesh and blood.

Growing up, I had an interesting family dynamic. I was born to a single mom and didn't know my biological dad. My mom and I lived with my grandparents until she married my stepdad when I was four years old. A baby brother was soon added to our family.

My Script:

My dad and I are so much alike that we just don't get along. We both want things done our way, and of course, I almost always lose, because I'm the kid, and he's the parent. We fight about really stupid things, like where our shoes should go, and our big thing is that my dad loves to tap me on the shoulder, and I really don't like to be touched, so I blow up at him, and then get into trouble. My family problems are nothing compared to a lot of other families, but the problems we have are still problems.
—Mallory, Arizona, age 15

We seem to never get along! I go through what seems like phases where I'm a great kid, and then I fight with my family a ton the next week. My parents and I fight about school—mostly grades, friends, how I am acting.
—Shelby, Iowa, age 15

Sometimes parents want me to be what they want me to be, and not who I really am.
—Robbie, Texas, age 14

Dealing with parents is hard enough, but in today's world "family" often includes divorced parents and step-parents, and various related family members. It's hard not to feel partly rejected or left out. It's hard not to wish that relationships could be better.

On the flipside of that, sometimes we're partly to blame for strained relationships. I know that was my problem, especially as a teen. I would complain that my parents didn't trust me, but I did nothing to earn their trust. (In fact, I'd do just the opposite.)

I'd feel left out and upset that no one paid attention to me, but whenever possible I spent my time with boyfriends or friends. And when I wasn't at someone else's house, I was on the phone planning the next get-together.

More than that, I viewed my parents as the enemy who hindered me from having fun. From having a "real" life. I didn't stop and consider whether the fun I wanted to have was truly in my best interest, or what God would want me to do. And, instead of listening, I usually found ways to do what I wanted, despite their attempts to reign me in.

FADE IN:

INT. LIVING ROOM
OF HOUSE—EVENING—
ESTABLISHING

TRISH VALLEY, 16, is
eating her dinner in
front of the TV. The
phone RINGS, and she
answers it.

> **TRISH**
> Hello?

> **CHASE**
> Hey, a group of
> us are getting
> together. My
> parents are out
> of town, and my
> older brother got
> us some beer.

> **TRISH**
> Can't do that. I'm
> still grounded for
> staying out too
> late last week.

> **CHASE**
> What time do
> your parents go
> to bed?

My Script:

The biggest thing I have a
problem with is that my parents always say that they
know what I'm going through
and they were my age once.
When that is mostly true,
they were my age like forever
ago! They don't get the world
these days and they don't
know even a portion of the
evil and the pressure to do
things that are wrong.
—Sarah, Colorado, age 15

I know that a lot of teens
believe their parents don't
understand them, and they're
right . . . to an extent. They
grew up in a different time
period, and they might not
understand a lot of things
that go on in our lives . . . but
they were also teens once
too. They had to deal with
some of the stuff we do.
—Leslie, Montana, age 14

My parents love me for who I
am. Unrealistic expectations
don't exist as far as I am
concerned. I always brag that
I have the coolest parents
ever, and I do!
—Sophie, Texas, age 14

Trish glances to her PARENTS, noting her
mother's gaze, and she knows her mom is
listening. Trish turns her back to her
mom and faces the wall.

> TRISH
> I don't know. In a couple hours I
> suppose.

> CHASE
> Okay, I'll be there around 11:30
> to pick you up. Your dad hasn't
> fixed that screen on the window yet,
> has he?

> TRISH
> Uh, no. Same place?

> CHASE
> Yeah, meet you at the end of the
> street.

> TRISH (louder)
> Fine, good. Talk to you tomorrow.

Trish watches TV with her parents and
then finally heads to her room after her
parents go to bed. She dresses in jeans
and a T-shirt, then watches the clock. At
11:30 she climbs from the window and JOGS
down the street toward Chase's car waiting
at the end of the road. CHASE meets her
halfway, and then they walk toward the
car. As they near it, another CAR

APPROACHES. Before they have a chance to climb in Chase's car, lights of a police car flash.

> **TRISH**
> I'm dead.

> **CHASE**
> Don't worry. We can talk our way out of it.

> **TRISH**
> Are you kidding? My dad's a cop, Chase. All the cops around here know me. And we're like a quarter of a mile from my house. My dad's going to find out for sure.

The police car stops, and the POLICE OFFICER approaches.

> **POLICE OFFICER**
> Heading somewhere, Trish?

> **TRISH**
> Uh, no. My friend just stopped by to talk. He was just heading home. I was just about to walk back to my house.

> **POLICE OFFICER**
> And you both know curfew was over an hour ago, right?

Trish nods.

> **CHASE**
> Yes, I'm really sorry, officer.

> **POLICE OFFICER**
> Good, and since you're heading home
> anyway, why don't I just join you? I
> think I'd like to talk to your dad,
> Trish.

The police officer turns to Chase.

> **POLICE OFFICER**
> And why don't you join us, young man?
> I'm sure Trish's dad would like to
> talk to you too.

> **CHASE**
> Yes, sir.

They head to the house, the police officer
leading the way. Chase leans close to
Trish to whisper in her ear.

> **CHASE** (whispering)
> We're both dead.

FADE OUT

There are a lot of parenting books that tell parents how to cope
with kids, but rarer are ones that teach kids how to cope with

parents. So my first piece of advice would be to NOT try anything similar to the script above. It's bad enough being disciplined and grounded, but it's even worse trying to sneak around it. Instead, here are a few other things you *can* do to improve your relationship with your parents:

Be respectful. Parents appreciate respect, especially dads. They live in a world where adults (for the most part) act in respectful ways. Sometimes it's hard to be respectful if you don't feel like anyone is listening to your point of view, but the more respect you give, the more you'll get in return.

Give encouragement. It's tough being a parent. I mean, how would you like to deal with all that they have to deal with on a daily basis? Encourage them when you see them tired or worn out. It may seem like something simple, but encouragement will go a long way.

Share your thoughts. Though they've gotten pretty good at reading your facial expressions, parents cannot read thoughts. Let them know how you feel about everything—the good, the bad, the ugly, the exciting. The

My Script:

I absolutely love my family and hope that many things are the same when I have a family, but there are a few things that I would change. I would want my kids to have a little more freedom to have fun than I have had. I also want my kids to be closer than my sisters and I were while growing up. Even though we are really close now, we weren't always the best of friends while we were younger.
—Melanie, Texas, age 17

Actually, talking to your parents helps conflict. Sometimes a parent just can't know what's going on in your head; after all, they aren't psychics. The bad thing is when a parent refuses to listen to you, and therefore remains ignorant to your thoughts and runs the risk of even more painful problems.
—Anna, Texas, age 14

I think that the only thing to help them understand better is for me to tell them about the things that are going on; go into a little more detail, and try to better explain things.
—Mallory, Arizona, age 15

more you help to open up lines of communication, the easier it will be to talk about all types of things, including things like unrealistic expectations. (And what parent doesn't have those?!)

Also, if you have something you want to talk about, but are afraid to do it face-to-face, consider e-mail, IM, or even a note. Sometimes it's easier to share your heart when you're not looking into your parent's eyes.

Strive for obedience. I don't have much to say about this (obviously!), except that my life was SO much easier when I obeyed my parents. Not only did we get along better, I truly feel God blessed my obedience. After all, He's not shy about talking about the importance of honoring your mom and dad. Just check out these verses:

> Children, obey your parents in every-
> thing, for this pleases the Lord.
> (Colossians 3:20)

> Children, obey your parents in the Lord,
> for this is right. "Honor your father and
> mother"—which is the first commandment
> with a promise—"that it may go well with
> you and that you may enjoy long life on
> the earth." (Ephesians 6:1-3)

> Listen, my son, to your father's instruc-
> tion and do not forsake your mother's
> teaching. (Proverbs 1:8)

There are tons more verses like these, and some get even a bit more colorful in their warnings. Listen to this one:

> The eye that mocks a father, that scorns
> obedience to a mother, will be pecked out

by the ravens of the valley, will be eaten by the vultures. (Proverbs 30:17)

Yikes!

It would be hard to give 100 percent obedience and respect, and that's why there is one other important aspect on dealing with parents:

Seek Forgiveness. If you've done something wrong, admit it. Hiding the truth only makes matters worse.

Another good thing about seeking forgiveness is that it's humbling. Sometimes I'll consider doing something I shouldn't, and if I know I'll most likely confess later, it *keeps me* from being disobedient in the first place. Humbling oneself and asking for forgiveness is a great hindrance from doing the wrong thing in the first place.

All the above works for brothers, sisters, and other family members too. In fact, who *wouldn't* like to be treated this way?

Take time to think about all your family relationships. Which ones do you enjoy the most?

My Script:

The love that we all share. We're always messing with each other, joking around and making each other "mad." It's so easy to go to my mom, or sometimes my dad (some things you just can't discuss with a guy), when I need something. My sisters are always there for me, there to hug me and play with me, and also to give me someone I HAVE to keep an eye on!
—Anna, Texas, age 14

My parents really trust me in almost everything, and they let me make most of my decisions. Most teens need this space to grow up and root themselves as individuals.
—Sarah, Colorado, age 15

My parents expect me to be perfect by studying for endless hours, to get good grades, eat right, have no one mad at me, get enough sleep, do my chores, watch my mouth, and SO MUCH MORE!!
—Lauren, Pennsylvania, age 14

my life, unscripted

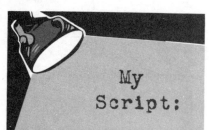

My Script:

It's not a great feeling when someone so close to you no longer trusts you. I was willing to do anything to get it back. I did my chores without arguing, and I tried to spend time with them as much as possible. I knew they had forgiven me, but that didn't mean I had gotten the trust back. It took a long time, but I have gained some of it back.

—Hannah, Texas, age 15

God's my Father, so when I'm with other Christians, I feel at home. With some people it's like finding a long lost relative and having to get used to them. Others, it's like finding out your worst enemy is your brother!

—Anna, Texas, age 14

As a part of a family, you don't want to bring disgrace to the family name so you should always think about your decision before you act upon it. When you are a Christian, you are a part of a very big family and you want to make sure that all of your actions and words bring Glory to God and not disgrace. (However, this is a lot easier said than done! But that doesn't mean we can't try our best!)

—Melanie, Texas, age 17

What do you like about them? What can you do to make them even better?

Also, consider which ones need work. How can *you* change in an effort to help the relationship? What types of changes would you pray for in the other person? In what ways would these changes honor God?

Finally, think about family situations that cause the most conflict. Why do they cause conflict? What could you do next time to help the situation? Script your answer (and your future actions) below.

Intermission

In addition to our earthly family, from the moment we accept Christ into our lives, we are adopted into a heavenly family of believers. While for the most part this is great, there are also varied personalities that can get in the way of truly caring for each other. What to do?

1. Realize that just as people act, believe, and think differently in families, they do in God's family too. In fact, if you read the New Testament, you'll discover that most books discuss conflict between Christians. God knew the problems we humans would have, and He made sure we had the answers ahead of time!

- Want to know how to act as a Christian? Colossians 3:1–14
- Struggling with sin? Romans 7 talks about that.
- Facing temptations? James 1:2–18

Whatever your problem is, the answer is in there!

2. Understand that different family members approach God in different ways. Some like quiet prayer and others love loud, exciting group worship. This, too, is okay.

3. Know that the closer you get to God, the easier it is to deal with family members—both in the church and at home. When praying for a family member, God often changes us in the process . . . and His changes are always right on!

18.
The Worst Horror Movie Ever
(facing your fears)

Films from the **horror** genre are designed to elicit fright, fear, terror, disgust or horror from viewers. In horror film plots, evil forces, events, or characters, sometimes of supernatural origin, intrude into the everyday world.[1]

I clearly remember the night I finished reading the book *Pet Cemetery* by Stephen King. The story is about animals (and people!) who come back to life after being buried in a sacred burial ground. I slept with my bedroom light on for a week, and I wouldn't let my cat come near me for even longer. It was the same cat who slept on my bed every night since seventh grade. Needless to say, the poor kitty was confused. According to him, life hadn't changed. It looked exactly the same on the outside. But something had changed—my thoughts and emotions. Because of a story, fear rooted itself into my thoughts and dug in deep. Trepidation took hold and wasn't about to let go.

Of course, even when fear coursed through my veins, I knew it was all because of a book. I found the cause of the angst, and I promised myself I'd never read a book like that again.

Worse yet is when there are situations in our lives that

make us afraid. These are the events that we wish would just go away. They grip us in such a solid state of fright.

One thing about fear is that it greatly hinders our decision-making skills. It's as if we're looking through the world with dark, dark glasses. Everywhere we turn we see no hope, and like a person left in a pitch-dark room, we start groping around, trying to find something to cling to.

It was during a truly fear-filled time in my life that I made one of my worse decisions ever. Numerous scenes in this book share about my experiences as a pregnant teen, but the ones shared so far are those where I made the right choice—to have my baby. A year and a half before that, at fifteen, I had also found myself pregnant. Fear wrapped securely around my heart and mind and wouldn't let go. Those dark shades tinted my view of everything around me, and I had no hope. Stumbling, I grasped at what seemed like an easy out, and I made a bad choice. A very bad choice. Proverbs 14:12 says:

> There is a way that seems right to a man,
> but in the end it leads to death.

Sin led to death, all right, but not for me . . . for the child I carried. It's a decision I've regretted ever since. One I can never take back. A decision caused by a fear that gripped me more strongly than any horror story.

FADE IN:

INT. SMALL OFFICE OF CLINIC—AFTERNOON— ESTABLISHING

TRISH VALLEY, 15, sits across from a CLINIC WORKER. The walls of the office are covered with posters with information

about various types of birth control and
facts about STDs. The clinic worker's
gaze is intent on Trish's face, but Trish
turns away. Instead, she focuses on her
trembling hands folded on her lap.

> **CLINIC WORKER**
> Well, you found out last week that
> you were pregnant. Have you had a
> chance to think about it? Talk to
> your boyfriend?

> **TRISH**
> Yeah, a little.

> **CLINIC WORKER**
> You seem pretty scared, alone. I'd
> like to help, but first there are a
> few things you need to know.

> **TRISH**
> Okay.

The clinic worker pulls some papers out of
her desk and places them before Trish.

> **CLINIC WORKER**
> Here is some information about
> pregnancy. About the difficulty teen
> moms have in life if they decide to
> continue on with their pregnancy,
> especially those your age. But this
> doesn't have to be the end of your
> life. Have you thought about
> termination?

TRISH
An abortion? Yeah, that's what my boyfriend wants me to do. His parents too.

CLINIC WORKER
That's something to take into consideration. If you carry to term, not only will your life completely change, but his will too. And you're both young. There are plenty of years ahead of you to think about having kids.

TRISH (hesitantly)
I just don't know.

CLINIC WORKER
I know it sounds scary, but it's a simple procedure. And you're not very far along. It's just like scraping a blob of tissue from inside you. Then you can continue on with everything as you know it. You can plan a good life and become better prepared for this type of commitment in the future.

TRISH
It's not a baby yet?

CLINIC WORKER
Not for many more months. It's just the same as scraping cells off the inside of your cheek. I think it's

the right choice for you. Then you
can continue on with school like
nothing ever happened. I know many
people who have terminated, and they
are very glad they did.

Trish's hands tremble even more, and
she crosses her arms over her chest. She
looks away, toward the wall of posters,
disconnecting herself from the words she's
about to say.

>   **TRISH** (distant)
>   Okay, that's what I want to do.

FADE OUT

FEAR GRIPS YOU

It was hard writing this scene, even many years after the fact.
Just typing these words caused my stomach to knot up and
my chest to ache. At that time I had many fears—the fear of
having to be responsible, the fear of losing my life as I knew
it, the fear of losing my boyfriend, and the fear of people
learning I was pregnant and looking down on me. When the
clinic worker offered what seemed to be a way out, I took it.
(I later found out that a twelve-week-old fetus has a beating
heart and formed body!) Little did I know the pain, shame,
and regret I'd have for the rest of my life.

Though it was hard, I shared this script for one purpose—

to give an example about how our decision making is clouded when our minds are filled with fear. We don't think straight, and we search for easy answers. We want help, and we'll grasp at anything that looks as if it might offer it.

I hope that your fears aren't quite as life changing, but they will affect you just the same. You fear a bad grade, so you may cheat. You fear losing your boyfriend, so you allow yourself to become sexually active with him. You fear not finding a boyfriend, so you dress and act in ways that draw the attention of guys—no matter if that's not how you really are on the inside.

Do you remember a time when fear motivated you, or someone you're close to, to make a bad decision? When? What happened?

Fear is an amazing motivator, yet the decisions that come out of it usually result in sin and pain, and sometimes even death. The truth is (as I mentioned early in this book), when you allow something or someone to motivate you, you become a slave to that thing or person. And in daily life we're either a slave to sin or a slave to God—there is no middle ground.

> Don't you know that when you offer your-
> selves to someone to obey him as slaves,
> you are slaves to the one whom you obey—
> whether you are slaves to sin, which
> leads to death, or to obedience, which
> leads to righteousness? But thanks be to
> God that, though you used to be slaves
> to sin, you wholeheartedly obeyed the

My Script:

I have always been afraid of failing. The problem is I take on so many extra activities that it becomes easy to fall behind in various aspects of my life. In fact, just recently, I was terrified that I was going to be kicked out of Student Council because I didn't get enough service hours in for the semester (mainly because of a drawn-out illness).

—Sarah, Indiana, age 15

When we go to God and ask, He gives peace. There have been plenty of times when I have been scared to death of petty things, and times when I have been nervous about stuff, and God never fails to bring me peace. It doesn't mean that everything will work out how we want, but it does mean that He will give peace and comfort us.

—Melanie, Texas, age 17

form of teaching to which you were entrusted. (Romans 6:16–17)

Thankfully, as this Scripture says, you can make a different choice. Even if you screwed up big time like I did, you can make a decision to follow God, *turning away* from the path that leads to death, *turning toward* the path that leads to life—eternal life.

FEAR NOT

There are many things in this life to be afraid of. Just listen to the evening news for fifteen minutes and you'll get an earful! Yet no matter what is going on in our lives, God is there. Not only that, He tells us NOT to fear. Why? Surely, God knows that things in our world are scary. But even more than that, He knows He has the situation under control. We do not know how big our God is, until we see Him as bigger than all our fears. We do not know true peace, until we feel God's presence in the middle of a storm. Difficult, fearful things will come into our lives, but it is there that we will know God better than we ever have before.

There are hundreds of verses that talk about not fearing, but here are two of my favorites:

The Worst Horror Movie Ever

> The LORD is my light and my salvation—
>   whom shall I fear?
> The LORD is the stronghold of my life—
>   of whom shall I be afraid?
> (Psalm 27:1)

> I sought the LORD, and he answered me;
> he delivered me from all my fears.
> Psalm 34:4)

Think about the things you fear. They could be things you're facing now, or things you are worried about in the future. What are those things?

Now, imagine those things in the palms of God's hands. Imagine Him in control of them. Look to His face. Can you see the peace He has? (After all, *He* knows how loving and powerful He is. He knows they are under His control.)

In the future, this will be a good image to come back to when you are afraid. It's also good to make a plan now for how you will handle fearful things in the future.

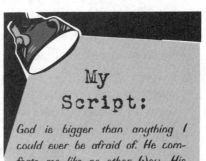

My Script:

God is bigger than anything I could ever be afraid of. He comforts me like no other. Wow. His grace is like a warm wave of peace.

—Sophia, Texas, age 14

When I am fearful, I pray that God will give me confidence to know that I'm never alone, and that His presence would wrap around me, and comfort me. And after I pray these things, it happens. God always comes through for me.

—Mallory, Arizona, age 15

Use the space below to answer this question: The next time I am afraid, I will . . .

Doesn't having a plan help? Especially when your plan is centered around your heavenly Father who loves you more than you can even imagine.

 Intermission

There is another side of fear, and it has nothing to do with horror movies. Instead, there is a wholesome fear that keeps us from doing what is dangerous or harmful. Fear of falling keeps us from hanging out too close to the edge of a cliff. Fear of addiction (and our parents' wrath!) keeps us from drinking or trying drugs. Fear of flunking out of high school keeps us from skipping classes. It also is a good motivator for doing our homework.

The Bible talks a lot about what we should not be afraid of, but it also talks about what (who) we should fear. Check out these verses:

> But be sure to fear the LORD and serve him faithfully with all your heart; consider what great things he has done for you. (1 Samuel 12:24)

> For the sake of your name, O LORD,
>   forgive my iniquity, though it is great.

My Script:

Fear can protect you from future regrets. Like if you get tempted to do something you shouldn't, fear can help you stay away from whatever it is.

—Shelby, Iowa, age 15

Sometimes, we need a fear of something so we don't underestimate that thing or things. It's when we let that fear keep us from living and doing what we need to do that it gets dangerous.

—Anna, Texas, age 14

Fear of God is a good thing. There is also a healthy fear that keeps you from doing stupid things.

—Miranda, Georgia, age 16

I fear turning away from God. Being in high school, there's a lot of peer pressure, and Christians don't exactly fit in too well. I fear that I'll turn my back on God, and I won't look back. I fear losing God, and so that is what I pray for most. Fear of the Lord is good, to respect, and love Him. To show surrender to Him, and that is the only time I think fear is good.

—Mallory, Arizona, age 15

Who, then, is the man that fears the LORD?
   He will instruct him in the way
     chosen for him.
He will spend his days in prosperity,
   and his descendants will inherit the land.
(Psalm 25:11-13)

Many times we focus on God's love and care, and we forget that God is holy and just. The fear here is not trembling in our boots, or the terror we get from horror movies. Instead, it is a holy reverence. It understands that sin separates us from God, and God will discipline those He loves in order to draw us back to Him and His ways. Hebrews 12:10 says:

> Our fathers disciplined us for a little while as they thought best; but God disciplines us for our good, that we may share in his holiness.

Take time to think about God's holiness. God is perfect and without sin. Consider how someday every person will have to stand before God and have his or her deeds judged. Does this cause fear and reverence to rise within?

Now consider ways you can carry this fear and reverence into your daily life. Jot your ideas here.

19.

Character Arc
(a new and different person)

A **character arc** is the status of the character as it unfolds throughout the story, the storyline, or series of episodes. Since the definition of character arc centers on the character, it is generally equated as the emotional change of the character within the narrative. Characters begin the story with a certain viewpoint and, through events in the story, that viewpoint changes. Often this change is for the better, but it can also be for the worse or simply different.[1]

In every movie there is a change in the character. Most of the time the change is for the good. In the movie *13 Going on 30*, Jenna (played by Jennifer Garner) learns she had the wrong goals about love and life. She discovers that what she wants most is the friendship she had when she was thirteen—something she had given up for popularity and a powerful career.

In *Ever After*, Prince Henry's eyes are opened to the cares of the citizens of his kingdom through the passionate concern of Danielle (aka Cinderella). I'm sure if you consider your favorite movies, you will see transformation in those characters too. In fact, we're disappointed if we *don't* see some type of change for the better.

Think about your character arc since beginning your journey through this book. Have you seen a change in the way you think? Have you discovered things deep in your

My Script:

One of my bad habits I've overcome is interrupting people. I used to just put in my thoughts before people had finished theirs. Now I listen.
—Lauren, Pennsylvania, age 14

I used to struggle with listening to gossip. No matter how much I hate gossip, I always tended to cling to every detail. I hated that I had become so consumed by gossip that I would hang around people just to get the juicy scoop. Then I realized that what I was doing was against God's law. Now, I could care less who is going out with who.
—Hannah, Texas, age 15

I pray a lot when I'm trying to overcome something. Praying helps me settle down, get to know myself, and get to love myself. I like to give my problems to Him, and He always helps.
—Anna, Texas, age 14

heart that you truly want most of all?

Take a few minutes and flip back through these pages. Think about the scripts you've written for your future. Has there been an emotional change that has happened within? What about a heart change? In what way?

Through the story of our lives, it is important that our character arc continually leads us closer to God, rather than away from Him. Over the story of *your* life, there will be small changes. Nothing, after all, stays the same.

It will be up to you from this point on to make sure they are the best changes for you. As you've learned, it is possible to think through and script your actions ahead of time, instead of just reacting to the choices of others and going with the flow.

Sometimes you'll simply strengthen your resolve to do what's right. Other times you'll work on getting rid of bad habits. Not every situation that comes into your life is worthy of a scene in a teen movie (thank goodness!), yet God is as concerned with the daily struggles as much as the biggies. They, too, are part of your character arc.

What are some of the bad habits you've overcome in the past?

My Script:

If I'm trying to overcome a habit, I work at it really hard. Usually if I have to break a habit, I wear a piece of jewelry and it will remind me that I shouldn't give in to the habit.
—Sarah, Minnesota, age 14

I want to become more of a girl who shows people Christ through her actions. I want to rely on God for absolutely EVERYTHING! Jesus needs to be first in my life.
—Sophie, Texas, age 14

What helped you to overcome them?

ADDING ON

In every movie there are a few things a character must give up in order to reach his/her goal. It's also important to consider what things we need to add on. In 2 Peter 1:5–9 (THE MESSAGE) we read:

> So don't lose a minute in building on what you've been given, complementing your basic faith with good character, spiritual understanding, alert discipline, passionate patience, reverent wonder, warm friendliness, and generous love, each dimension fitting into and developing the others. With these qualities active and growing in your lives, no grass will grow under your feet, no day will pass without its reward as you mature in your experience of our Master Jesus. Without these qualities you can't see what's right before you, oblivious that your old sinful life has been wiped off the books.

Look over the godly traits listed below that are added on to basic faith. Circle the ones you would like to work on first. Then beside it script just how you will add on or grow in this way.

good character

spiritual understanding

alert discipline

passionate patience

reverent wonder

warm friendliness

generous love

FADE IN:

INT. BEDROOM—MORNING—ESTABLISHING

TRISH VALLEY, 17, hears her BABY'S soft COO-
ING. She rises and looks into the bassinet.
A small baby boy kicks his legs. She picks
him up and places a kiss on his cheek.

> **TRISH**
> Let's go see if Grandma will watch
> you so Mommy can take a shower, okay?

Trish walks into the kitchen where her MOM
is POURING herself a bowl of cereal.

> **TRISH**
> Mom, can you watch him for a few
> minutes so I can take shower?

> **MOM** (surprised)
> You're going to church today? Of
> course I can hold him. Come here,
> buddy.

Trish hands the baby to her mom.

> **TRISH**
> Yeah, I'm going to start going,
> regularly. And I've been reading
> my Bible too.

> **MOM**
> That's wonderful. I've really seen a
> change in you.

TRISH
Well, it took a little shaking up
in my life for me to realize what's
important. But now that I have, I
don't want to lose it.

Trish leans over and places a kiss on her
baby, then hurries to the shower. She
glances in the mirror and smiles.

TRISH (whispering)
Yeah, I see a change too. A good
change. Thank you, God.

FADE OUT

EVALUATE

Scripting your life doesn't have to be something you stop
once you put away this book. All through your life it will
help you make good decisions if you evaluate what's working and what's not. It also helps if you take time to note your
emotions too.

Do you feel anxious? Anxiety may mean you're doing
something you shouldn't. Or the opposite of that, it could
mean you need to do something you're afraid to do. Are you
depressed? That could mean you're looking for happiness
from things of this world and not looking for true joy from
God. Are you worried? Maybe you're focusing on everything

My Script:

By evaluating my life, I've learned that I haven't done much with it. Sure, I've made friends, but I haven't done much of the things that count. From now on I'm going to try to be more like Him.

—Anna, Texas, age 14

Evaluating my life gives me insight. Knowing where I need growth, where I need change, what I need to be doing differently, or even what I'm doing right.

—Miranda, Georgia, age 16

By evaluating my life, I have gained the view of an outsider. It helps me to be able to accept my little faults, and correct my larger ones.

—Lauren, Pennsylvania, age 14

you can't control instead of realizing God *does* have everything in control. Not only that, Jesus is there to free you from those cares.

Right now is a good time to start. Consider what is happening in your life. Think about your emotions and how you are responding to things. Evaluate what you need to give up or add on, and jot those down in the space below.

THE ULTIMATE

Of course the ultimate goal of evaluating your life and taking time to script your future actions and responses is to deepen your relationship with God. How has your relationship changed since you've embarked on your journey through this book?

What other changes would you like to see in the near future?

What are three small steps that could get you moving in the right direction?

1.

2.

3.

Start with those.

My
Script:

My relationship with God has grown, and now I feel strength, happiness, and have a feeling of being protected. Strength because I know that He will help me, or be with me when I need Him, or when I just want to talk. Happiness because I am with my Father! How couldn't I be happy? And feeling protected, because I know He is with me every step of the way.
—Lauren, Pennsylvania, age 14

In my growing relationship with God, I have gained a lot of wisdom and love. I can honestly say that now when I make a decision, I base it on faith in my God.
—Sarah, Minnesota, age 14

One word. Confidence.
—Robbie, Texas, age 14

I have gained a better life and a better conscience. When God works through me, I feel more . . . alive and more real. Jesus shows me a side of life that I normally do not see. God is amazing and can do the impossible! He helps me understand the unthinkable.
—Sophia, Texas, age 14

God gives me a sense of closure and peace about things that I did wrong and mistakes I had made.
—Hannah, Texas, age 15

Intermission

Every small step either leads us toward God or away. Listen to what Psalm 119:1–3 (THE MESSAGE) says:

You're blessed when you stay on course,
walking steadily on the road revealed by
GOD. You're blessed when you follow his
directions, doing your best to find him.
That's right—you don't go off on your own;
you walk straight along the road he set.

This Scripture continues on. In fact, it's a perfect prayer to pray daily! Find a piece of paper or a few note cards and write this down. Then post it someplace you'll see it often. It only takes one minute to pray this prayer, but, oh, what a difference it can make in your heart, attitude, and life!

You, GOD, prescribed the right way to live;
    now you expect us to live it.
Oh, that my steps might be steady,
    keeping to the course you set;
Then I'd never have any regrets
    in comparing my life with your counsel.
I thank you for speaking straight from your heart;
    I learn the pattern of your righteous ways.
I'm going to do what you tell me to do;
    don't ever walk off and leave me.
How can a young person live a clean life?
    By carefully reading the map of your Word.
I'm single-minded in pursuit of you;
    don't let me miss the road signs you've posted.
I've banked your promises in the vault of my heart
    so I won't sin myself bankrupt.
Be blessed, GOD;
    train me in your ways of wise living.
I'll transfer to my lips
    all the counsel that comes from your mouth;
I delight far more in what you tell me about living
    than in gathering a pile of riches.

I ponder every morsel of wisdom from you,
     I attentively watch how you've done it.
I relish everything you've told me of life,
     I won't forget a word of it.
Be generous with me and I'll live a full life;
     not for a minute will I take my eyes off
     your road.
Open my eyes so I can see
     what you show me of your miracle-wonders.
(Psalm 119:4-18 THE MESSAGE)

20.
Climax
(moment of change)

cli·max *noun.* (in a dramatic or literary work) a decisive moment that is of maximum intensity or is a major turning point in a plot.[1]

The climax of the movie is the big event at the end where the character must make the choice between facing a challenge or walking away. Usually there is a great prize to be won—a race, a girl, self-respect. There are also obstacles in the way. Big obstacles, which result in a crisis. The climax isn't the crisis, but rather the action or emotion that comes from the character in response to the crisis.

There will be times in your life where you will face a crisis. Maybe you already have. Times of crisis will come to us all, yet it is the climax—your action or emotion that will make all the difference. Will you rise to the occasion? Will you step back in defeat? Will you walk away?

Think of times in your life where you've faced a crisis of sorts. Is there any time you followed through? Is there any time you walked away? Explain. How did your choice affect your life?

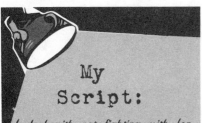

My Script:

I deal with not fighting with (or killing) my sisters, having a good time, being involved with other people, sharing my faith. All of these things are good to do, but amazingly hard!
—Anna, Texas, age 14

There are so many choices we face daily. Concerning friends, family, God, school, boys, and just life in general. We face questions like, What should I say? What should I do? What shouldn't I say or do?
—Miranda, Georgia, age 16

What to wear, how to act, where to go, who to go with, what to say. All those things aren't always easy. Especially the "what" to say part. I don't always say the nicest things. That's another thing I'm working on, saying the godly thing, and standing firm on my beliefs.
—Hannah, Texas, age 15

On a daily basis I make the choice of obeying my parents, listening to God, even telling boys that I really like that I can't be with them.
—Sarah, Minnesota, age 14

There are times in our lives where we *will* make big decisions, but for the most part it is the daily choices that will transform your life. Today, you can have a moment of change. Tomorrow too. Not big, giant steps, but tiny, baby steps that are always moving you in the right direction.

What choices do you have to make on a daily basis? How will your choices today affect your life tomorrow?

BOUNDARIES

Of course, as I've said a zillion times in this book (just a slight exaggeration), it helps so much if you think about your actions and responses ahead of time. In this case, it will help you make major (or minor) decisions if you set rules or boundaries for yourself. It also gives you time to seek God *before* you are in crisis mode. Isaiah 30:21 says:

Whether you turn to the right or to the left, your ears will hear a voice behind you, saying, "This is the way; walk in it."

Have you thought about what right choices you are determined to stick with, no matter what the cost? Has God made it clear which way you are to walk concerning some matters? Make a list of those things in the space below.

My Script:

I'm sticking with my morals and beliefs. To please God in all ways—body, soul, mind, heart, and spirit. So whatever right choices I have to make to please God are the choices I'm determined to stick with.
—Miranda, Georgia, age 16

I'm staying pure until marriage, not drinking or doing drugs ever!! Not laying my beliefs aside just to make sure someone doesn't get their feelings hurt.
—Hannah, Texas, age 15

I've decided to stick with God. I need to make the best God choice I can make. A God choice being a choice that would make Him smile, not frown.
—Lauren, Pennsylvania, age 14

THE CLIMAX
(THE FINAL ONE!)

cli·max *noun.* the highest or most intense point in the development or resolution of something; culmination.[2]

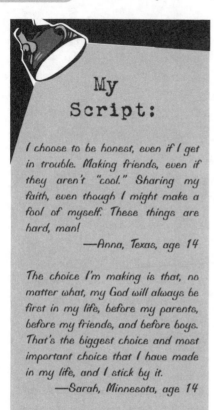

My Script:

I choose to be honest, even if I get in trouble. Making friends, even if they aren't "cool." Sharing my faith, even though I might make a fool of myself. These things are hard, man!

—Anna, Texas, age 14

The choice I'm making is that, no matter what, my God will always be first in my life, before my parents, before my friends, and before boys. That's the biggest choice and most important choice that I have made in my life, and I stick by it.

—Sarah, Minnesota, age 14

Wow, we've talked about so much in these twenty chapters. We've really dug deep, and we've made BIG plans. Yet sometimes analyzing and planning and dreaming gets a little overwhelming. If you're like me, it helps to realize that we will be rewarded for our effort.

Rewards are a part of life. We study, and we get an A. We clean our room, and we get allowance. We save up our money, and we get to buy something special. We obey God, and He has an awesome reward in store for us.

You see, there is another definition of the word *climax*. I've given it above. And while it is AWESOME to walk with God on earth, the climax of our Christian experience will be meeting Him someday face-to-face.

Can you imagine that?

All the other scripts in this book about Trish Valley have been struggles I've faced in the past. While they were great tools for learning (at least *I hope* you learned from my mistakes), I'd like to glimpse into a scene in the future. Won't you join me?

FADE IN:
EXT. HEAVEN—DAY—ESTABLISHING

TRISH is standing before the heavenly
throne. As far as she can see in every
direction are OTHERS with their hands
lifted WORSHIPING God. Joy and beauty fill
their faces. Trish feels a hand on her
shoulder and turns. Her face brightens as
she sees YOU. She opens her arms and pulls
you into her embrace.

> **TRISH**
> Oh, I've been waiting all this time
> to meet you!

> **YOU**
> Really? But how did you know? I was
> just someone who read your book when
> I was a teenager.

> **TRISH** (chuckling)
> It's amazing how much I know up
> here. That was a hard book to write.
> It was so real and raw. I asked myself
> if I was completely crazy writing
> those hard things . . . but you know
> what? I can't even remember what those
> things were. I remember those were
> some hard teen years, but the memory
> of them is gone. In fact, that life on
> earth seems like just one breath after
> all we've experienced so far. I can't
> wait to see what else the rest of
> eternity has in store for us.

You nod your head and gaze around.
You are in awe even though it seems
as if you've been here forever.

YOU (in awe)
This is what it was all about, wasn't
it? Deepening my relationship with
God. The whole secret of God's message was Christ in us. And now,
because of that, we are here with
Christ.

TRISH
So, can you tell me more? I'd love
to hear your story. You had a wonderful script, and I'd love to hear how
God used it to draw you to Him.

YOU
Of course! I can't wait to tell you.
God is so good. He was faithful to
me every step of the way. I love
thanking Him for that.

TRISH
Then let's do that now. After all, we
have all eternity to talk.

Together you and Trish turn toward the
throne, and you lift your arms in praise,
joining the CHORUS of praises flowing from
the lips of those whose stories centered
around this very throne.

NO FADING OUT

ETERNAL SCRIPT

Yes, friend, that is what we get to look forward to! Of course, it is a poor attempt to explain something that *will* be amazing. It's not my fault, of course. No mind can comprehend it! Look at 1 Corinthians 2:9–10:

```
However, as it is written:
    "No eye has seen,
    no ear has heard,
    no mind has conceived
    what God has prepared for those who
        love him"—
but God has revealed it to us
        by his Spirit.
The Spirit searches all things,
    even the deep things
    of God.
```

What do you imagine heaven will be like?

How does it make you feel to know that you WILL be rewarded for *Your Life, Scripted*? Rewards aren't a bad thing, after all. God designed them for us, and they are a great motivator!

But even more than that, the greatest reward of heaven is the fact that we are *His* . . . forever! I just love what Max Lucado has to say about this:

> For all its peculiarities and unevenness, the Bible has a simple story. God made man. Man rejected God. God won't give up until he wins him back.
>
> God will whisper. He will shout. He will touch and tug. He will take away our burdens; he'll even take away our blessings. If there are a thousand steps between us and him, he will take all but one. But he will leave the final one for us. The choice is ours.
>
> Please understand. His goal is not to make you happy. His goal is to make you his. His goal is not to get you what you want; it is to get you what you need.[3]

God knows that what we need most is Him. And when we get God, we will have Him forever. That is the final climax we can look forward to. The culmination of everything we've lived for.

I can't wait to see you there!

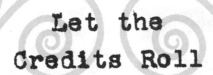

Let the Credits Roll

cred·it *noun.* an acknowledgment of work done, as in the production of a motion picture or publication.[1]

This book wouldn't be possible without the amazing teens who gave me advice, offered comments, answered questionnaires, and read these chapters for me! Their names are noted on the acknowledgements page, and they are the best!

Of course, the wisdom shared through me—and through them—only comes from one place, and that is Jesus Christ.

We are weak people, and even as I wrote some of this I thought to myself, *Yeah, great advice . . . maybe you should follow it 100 percent of the time.* I don't. No one can, but thankfully, in our weakness the power of God is truly shown! We see it in 2 Corinthians 12:9–10:

> But he said to me, "My grace is sufficient for you, for my power is made perfect in weakness." Therefore I will boast all the more gladly about my weaknesses, so that Christ's power may rest on me. That is why, for Christ's sake, I delight in weaknesses, in insults, in hardships, in persecutions, in difficulties. For when I am weak, then I am strong.

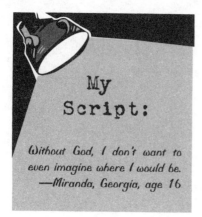

My Script:

Without God, I don't want to even imagine where I would be.
—Miranda, Georgia, age 16

Whatever you face in the days, weeks, and years to come, realize that Jesus's grace is sufficient for you. His power is perfect in weakness.

So when you mess up, turn to Him for strength.

But also remember, when you succeed—and when others notice the change in you—give credit where credit is due. None of your transformation would be possible without God who scripted our salvation and our future glory before the world began.

To Him be the glory, and honor, and praise for our lives, well scripted, and well lived!

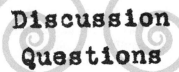

Discussion
Questions

1.
Not TV Land:
The Real Deal

Scripture References: Romans 3:23

1. At this point in your life, would you say your life "script" is a comedy, drama, horror, tragedy, or a thriller? Why?
2. Have you ever felt pressured to do something that made you feel uncomfortable? Did you go ahead and do it? Why or why not?
3. Have you ever found yourself in a "stupid" situation? (Something you wonder just *how* you got in the middle of???) If so, can you look back and seewhat were the steps that led you there? What were they?
4. In this chapter, I shared how I let my emotions have complete control over my behavior. What rules your "script"? Are you governed by your emotions or something else?
5. What are the top five struggles in your life? What causes these struggles—are they internal (inside) or external (outside) influences?
6. What role does God play in your script? Is He the director, a supporting role, or merely an extra?

2.
Dialogue:
The Way You Talk to Yourself

Scripture References: Psalms 139:14–17, Romans 3:27–28, Isaiah 55:8–12, Psalm 33:11, Psalm 40:5, Isaiah 46:10, Hosea 14:9

1. Think about how you've "talked to yourself" in the last few days. Would you say it is scripted or unscripted?

Discussion Questions

2. How does your self-talk affect your outward behavior?
3. Compare what you tell yourself with what God's Truth says. Are there some lies that you are telling yourself? Do you think you can stop believing those lies? How?
4. Do you believe God has a plan for your life? Based on the way you live your life, do your actions prove that you trust that God knows what's best for you?
5. Think about the time you spend in the Word. How does "being in the Word" direct your self-talk?

3.
Character Sketches:
All About You

Scripture References: Zephaniah 3:17, 2 Corinthians 5:17, Romans 6:6–14, Ephesians 2:1–5, Colossians 2:20

1. Compare the character you created in this chapter with the real you. Do you match up? In what ways are you/they different?
2. Has there been much conflict in your life? Do you think is has shaped who you are today? Is that a good or a bad thing? Both?
3. Do you feel confident about your abilities? Do you ever let other's opinion of you dictate how you feel/think about yourself?
4. Do you find it hard or easy to root for yourself in everyday life? Why?
5. What role do your friends play in how you feel about yourself? What about your parents? Siblings? God?

4.
On Location:
Here or There?

Scripture References: Hebrews 13:14, John 14:1–3, Romans 12:12, Colossians 3:2–3

1. When/where is the easiest time/place for you to feel close to

God? What are some ways to "take" that closeness with you during your day?

2. What places, or things, or people distract you from seeking God?
3. Do think that who you are changes with your setting?
   Are you different with your friends than with your parents?
   What about church and school? If so, why?
4. What motivates you to act in different ways? Who are you trying to please?
5. How can keeping an eternal perspective (realizing that your life is not just about this day, but about eternity) change the way you respond to God and others?

5.
Hero's Journey:
Popularity-Getting It and Keeping It for Real

Scripture References: Galatians 1:11, Galatians 1:15, Psalm 119, Jeremiah 29:13, Matthew 7:7–8

1. Is being popular important to you? Why or why not?
2. What is "true" popularity? Would you say that you are truly popular?
3. In what ways do you let other people's standard of "popularity" affect you?
4. Do you feel pressured to be one way or another?
5. How does your opinion of what is "cool" line up with the Bible's standard?

6.
Decision:
Preparing for Peer Pressure

Scripture References: Galatians 1:10, 2 Corinthians 7:23, Psalm 138:3

1. What type of peer pressure do you face? How does that affect the rest of your life?

2. How do you stay strong when others want you to do something you know you shouldn't? How can you mentally prepare yourself to stay strong in ANY situation?
3. How can God and His Word guide you through the pressures you face?
4. Are you a slave to anything in your life? Does anything have an unhealthy hold over you?
5. What do you base your decisions on? What or who has the most influence over you when making decisions?

7.
Inner Conflict:
Insecurity Is Something We Can Battle

Scripture References: Psalm 145:19, John 14:27, Proverbs 4:23

1. When are times you feel most insecure? What do you do to overcome those feelings?
2. Do you ever feel like you're the only one who doesn't have her act together?
3. Do you struggle with feeling like you're "enough"? How does that line up with God's promises?
4. What would you say your needs are? Do you think they are being filled?
5. What steps, if any, do you need to take to make God your go-to guy when you're feeling insecure, confused, or conflicted?

8.
Wardrobe:
Dressing Up

Scripture References: Romans 7:15–25, Galatians 5:22, 1 Samuel 16:7, Judges 6:34

1. How would you describe yourself? Do you think others would describe you the same way?

2. What can people tell about you from the outside?
3. Do you think you relate to others—through your words and actions—how you expect to be treated? Why or why not?
4. Think about your interactions with people over the last few weeks. Are there any pieces in your character wardrobe you need to get rid of?
5. Are you in need of a spiritual make-over? What would that look like? Describe the before and after photo.

9.
Blockbuster Buddies:
Everyone Deserves a Supporting Cast

Scripture References: Proverbs 17:17, Proverbs 22:24, Proverbs 16:28, Proverbs 18:19, Proverbs 25:11, Proverbs 25:13, Proverbs 27:9, Proverbs 27:17

1. What do you look for in a friend? Have you found that kind of friend?
2. Would you say you are a good friend? Why?
3. What role do your friends play in your life? Are they good influences or negative ones?
4. Do you find yourself relying on your friends more than relying on God?
5. Why do you think we need friends?

10.
The Hottie:
Need Someone to Play the Boyfriend Role?

Scripture References: Song of Solomon 2:7, 2 Corinthians 6:14–16

1. Do you feel pressured to have a boyfriend? Is it something that is important to you? Does it define who you are?
2. When you started dating, what were you hoping to find? Did you find it?

3. When it comes to dating, do you think boys and girls are both looking for the same things? What *are* they looking for?
4. Do you think dating is a good idea for you at this point in your life? Explain your opinion.
5. What sort of safeguards can you put in place to protect yourself when dating? What role does God have in dating?

11.
Admission:
What Does Beauty Cost?

Scripture References: 2 Peter 1:3–4, Proverbs 31:30–31, 1 Peter 3:3–5

1. Do you find yourself comparing your weaknesses to other people's strengths? How do you deal with this?
2. How does connecting with God help you when you find yourself internally keeping score?
3. Honestly, how does the media affect your image of yourself?
4. How does the image you have of yourself affect the way you live your life? Do you have any unhealthy habits that you need to stop or need help overcoming? What are they?
5. Does how you feel about yourself affect your relationships with other people?

12.
Villains:
People You Love to Hate

Scripture References: Matthew 5:43–47, John 15:18–19, Proverbs 15:1, James 1:26, 1 Timothy 1:5–6, 1 Peter 5:6–8

1. Most movies have villains. Who are the villains in your life?
2. How can God help you handle conflict with other people?
3. Who do you turn to for advice? Do you usually listen to their advice or follow your own?
4. Can conflict with others ever be a good thing? Do you think

conflict can teach you things about yourself and God?
Explain.

5. In your own life, how can planning ahead help you in times of conflict? What sort of responses can you script for current conflicts in your life?

13.
The Critic:
The Harshest Judge

Scripture References: Philippians 2:3–8, John 14:6

1. Do you struggle with criticism, criticizing yourself and others? In what ways?
2. What does your inner critic tell you? Is it in line with God's truth?
3. Do you think you are self-centered? Do you think others would agree with you?
4. Do you think others' criticism is ever a correct assessment of you? Has this ever happened? If so, how do you respond?
5. Do you ever criticize others to make yourself feel better? Does it work?

14.
The Mentor:
Wisdom When You Need It Most

Scripture References: Philippians 4:8, Ephesians 4:1–3, 2 Corinthians 6:14–18

1. Who do you turn to for advice? Why?
2. What does *wisdom* mean to you? Where do you find it?
3. Does the wisdom of God play a practical role in your life? Why or why not?
4. In the last year, would you say that you've grown closer to or farther away from God?
5. Do you consider the Bible a mentor in your own life?

15.
Fantasy:
Truly Out of This World

Scripture References: 1 Corinthians 4:1–2,
1 Corinthians 1:26–27, Colossians 2:2–3, John 3:16

1. Do you tend to take life too seriously or not seriously enough?
2. Do you ever hurt others by careless words or actions? When was the last time this happened?
3. What are your favorite types of movies or books? Does your life have those same types of stories?
4. Do you let God write the script of your life? Do you edit His efforts?
5. What role does trust play in your life-script?

16.
The Action and Adventure Movie:
Search for the Treasure

Scripture References: Ephesians 1:6, Matthew 6:31–33,
Psalms 16:11, Ephesians 6:10–18

1. If your life were like a fantasy plot, what would it be about?
2. What do you find yourself daydreaming about? Are your daydreams plans for the future or an escape?
3. Do you often find that your daydreams make you dissatisfied about real life? In what ways?
4. If your fantasies DID come true . . . would that be a good thing? Would they take you closer to God? Why or why not?
5. Is there anything that you are seeking that you shouldn't be? How do you separate the good from the bad?

17.
The Family Film:
Wholesome Entertainment . . . or Not!

Scripture References: Colossians 3:20, Ephesians 6:1–3,
Proverbs 1:8, Proverbs 30:17, Colossians 3:1–14, Romans 7,
James 1:2–18

1. What are your biggest family conflicts?
2. Do you feel like your parents sometimes don't understand you? What could help them understand you better?
3. Looking forward to the future, how would you like your future family to differ from your family now? What things are you thankful for in your family?
4. How does being a part of God's family make you think differently about the decisions you make?
5. Have you ever lost your parents' trust? How do you earn it back? Is it hard for you to ask for their forgiveness? Why or why not?

18.
The Worst Horror Movie Ever:
Facing Your Fears

Scripture References: Proverbs 14:12, Romans 6:16–17,
Psalm 27:1, Psalm 34:4, 1 Samuel 12:24, Psalm 25:11–13,
Hebrews 10:12

1. Sometimes bad things do happen—we lose people we love or things don't turn out as we had hoped. How do you deal with this?
2. How does God help when you are afraid? Who do you turn to first?
3. What do you fear most?
4. Is there ever a time when fear can be a good thing? How can fear of the Lord motivate you?
5. Has fear ever motivated you to do something you knew you shouldn't? What was the consequence? What did you learn?

19.
Character Arc:
A New and Different Person

Scripture References: 2 Peter 1:5–9, Psalm 119

1. How have you grown as a person in recent years? What has caused that growth?
2. What role does connecting with God have in your growth?
3. In what ways do you want or *need* to grow in the future?
4. Do you believe that God cares about your daily life—things like struggles, conflicts, chores, siblings? What in your life could you point to that proves your trust in God?
5. What would you say the purpose of your life is? What does God say it is? What does the world say it is? How do these three compare?

20.
Climax:
Moment of Change

Scripture Reference: Isaiah 30:21, 2 Corinthians 2:9–10

1. What bad habits have you kissed goodbye? Which ones still need some work?
2. What steps will you take to overcome those bad habits? What worked for you in the past?
3. The climax of the movie is the big event at the end where the character must make the choice between following through or walking away. What choices do you have to face on a daily basis? Are there any choices you are determined to stick with, no matter what cost?
4. Since you started this book, do you think you have grown in your relationship with God? What have you gained by doing so?
5. What have you gained by evaluating your life?

Giving Your Life to Jesus

When I gave my life to Christ, I didn't pray a fancy prayer, but I knew I wanted to seek Him and follow Him in all things. I knew Jesus loved me and had a good future planned for me. Your prayer doesn't have to be fancy either. In fact, it's as easy as A-B-C.

A—Accept that you are a sinner and that no matter how hard you try you could never do enough good things to earn your way into heaven and eternity with God.

B—Believe Jesus is God's Son. Believe He died on the cross as the penalty for your sins. Believe He rose again and desires a personal relationship with you.

C—Confess your sins and ask Jesus to be Lord of your life.

Your Prayer:

For all have sinned and fall short of the glory of God. Romans 3:23

If you confess with your mouth, "Jesus is Lord," and believe in your heart that God raised him from the dead, you will be saved. Romans 10:9

If we confess our sins, he is faithful and just and will forgive us our sins and purify us from all unrighteousness. 1 John 1:9

Repent, then, and turn to God, so that your sins may be wiped out, that times of refreshing may come from the Lord. Acts 3:19

You may wonder why I didn't include a prayer for you to repeat.

215

heart. Read through the Bible verses in the sidebar and think about them before you pray. Talk to God and tell Him that you believe Jesus is Lord and He died for your sins. Then just pray from your heart. God's listening. He wants nothing more than to have a personal relationship with you.

If you have accepted Christ for the first time, or you have rededicated yourself to Him, please let me know! Email me at MyLifeUnscripted@triciagoyer.com.

What's next?

Tell a Christian friend about your commitment.

Find a Bible-believing church to attend.

Read your Bible and connect with God throughout the day. Ask Him to help you script your life!

Acknowledgments

John, what a wild child you married! Thank you for loving me more than I even thought one person could.

Cory, Leslie, and Nathan. You've added fun and humor to the script of our home. I love it!

My loving family . . . Grandma, Mom, Dad, Ronnie—an awesome supporting cast.

Bruce, Susan, Stacey, Kimberley, Lesley, and Melissa—an unexpected twist to my story, but one greatly appreciated!

Amy Lathrop, my dear friend and everything-girl. Thanks!

My agent, Janet Kobobel Grant. An awesome mentor and guide.

The Thomas Nelson team . . . yeah to working with such amazing people once again.

My "unofficial" editors, Cara Putman, Amy Lathrop, Judy Gann. You're the best!

Finally, this book wouldn't be written if not for AMAZING teen girls who gave their input and answered all my many, many questions: Anna, Ashley G., Ashley R., Christa, Hannah Sn., Hannah So., Jayme, Katy, Laura S., Lauren, Leslie, Mallory, Mary Ellen, Melanie, Miranda, Pam, Robbie, Sarah M., Sarah W., Shelby K., Sophia, and Stephanie.

About the Author

TRICIA GOYER is the author of nine books, with three more to be released in 2007. She currently has five published novels with Moody Publishing and won Historical Novel of the Year in 2005 and 2006 from ACFW. She also won Writer of the Year from Mount Hermon Christian Writers Conference in 2003. And her book *Life Interrupted* was a finalist for the Gold Medallion in 2005. In addition to her novels, Tricia writes nonfiction books and magazine articles for publications like *Today's Christian Woman* and *Focus on the Family*. Tricia has one children's book *10 Minutes to Showtime* with Thomas Nelson. Tricia also speaks numerous times each year to women's groups, and has been a workshop presenter at the MOPS (Mothers of Preschoolers) International Convention.

Notes

Chapter 1
1. "Teenagers," Barna Research Online, www.barna.org.
2. *Dictionary.com Unabridged (v 1.0.1)*, s.v. "Storyboard," Dictionary.com, http://dictionary. reference.com/search?r=2&q= storyboard (accessed September 2, 2006).

Chapter 2
1. *WordNet® 2.1.*, Princeton University, s.v. "Dialogue," Dictionary.com, http://dictionary.reference.com/browse/dialogue (accessed January 26, 2007).
2. *Dictionary.com Unabridged (v 1.0.1)*, s.v. "Stage direction," Dictionary.com, http://dictionary.reference.com/search?r=2&q =stage direction (accessed September 3, 2006).

Chapter 3
1. *Webster's New Millennium™ Dictionary of English, Preview Edition (v 0.9.6)*, "Character sketch," Dictionary.com, http://dictionary.reference.com/browse/ character sketch (accessed January 26, 2007).

Chapter 4
1. *The American Heritage® Dictionary of the English Language*, 4th edition, "Location," Dictionary.com, http://dictionary. reference.com/browse/location (accessed January 26, 2007).
2. *WordNet® 2.1*, s.v. "Entertainment," Dictionary.com, http://dictionary.reference. com/browse/entertainment (accessed January 23, 2007).

Chapter 5
1. Need note for journey (see p. 45) journey. Dictionary.com. *Dictionary.com Unabridged (v 1.1)*. Random House, Inc. http://dictionary. reference.com/browse/journey (accessed: May 04, 2007).

2. *WordNet® 2.1*, s.v. "Popularity," Dictionary.com, http://dictionary.reference. com/browse/popularity (accessed January 26, 2007).

Chapter 6
1. *Dictionary.com Unabridged (v 1.1)*. Random House, Inc. http://dictionary. reference.com/browse/decision (accessed: May 04, 2007).
2. *Dictionary.com Unabridged (v 1.1)*, s.v. "Slave," Dictionary.com, http://dictionary. reference.com/browse/slave (accessed January 24, 2007).

Chapter 7
1. *WordNet® 2.1*, s.v. "Conflict," Dictionary.com, http://dictionary.reference. com/browse/conflict (accessed January 26, 2007).
2. America Ferrera quoted in "God Bless America" by Lori Berger, *Cosmogirl*, February 2007, 86–87.
3. Dictionary.com. *Dictionary.com Unabridged (v 1.1)*. Random House, Inc. http://dictionary.reference.com/browse/ insecurity (accessed: May 04, 2007).

Chapter 8
1. *Dictionary.com Unabridged (v 1.1)*, s.v. "Wardrobe," Dictionary.com, http://dictionary. reference.com/browse/wardrobe (accessed January 25, 2007).
2. Gregory A. Boyd, *Seeing Is Believing* (Grand Rapids, MI: Bake Books, 2004), 22–23.
3. Beth Moore, *Living Beyond Yourself*, Lifeway Christian Resources (Nashville, Tennessee), 24.

Chapter 9
1. s.v. "Cast list," http://trekweb.com/ Scriptwriting/terminology.html.

2. http://www.usaweekend.com/03_issues/
030420/030420teensurvey.html.
3. http://www.usaweekend.com/03_issues/
030420/030420teensurvey.html.

Chapter 10
1. *Dictionary.com Unabridged (v 1.1)*, s.v.
"Hero," Dictionary.com, http://dictionary.
reference.com/browse/hero (accessed
January 25, 2007).
2. http://www.teenpregnancy.org/resources/
data/pdf/TeenSexActivityOnePagerJune0.6.pdf.

Chapter 11
1. *Dictionary.com Unabridged (v 1.1)*, s.v.
"Admission," Dictionary.com, http://dictionary.
reference.com/browse/admission (accessed
February 21, 2007).

Chapter 12
1. *The American Heritage® Dictionary of
the English Language*, 4th edition, s.v.
"Villain," Dictionary.com,http://dictionary.
reference.com/browse/Villain (accessed
February 22, 2007).
2. *Dictionary.com Unabridged (v 1.1)*,
s.v. "Resolution," Dictionary.com, http://
dictionary.reference.com/browse/resolution
(accessed February 22, 2007).

Chapter 13
1. *Dictionary.com Unabridged (v 1.1)*, s.v.
"Critic," Dictionary.com, http://dictionary.
reference.com/browse/critic (accessed
February 23, 2007).

Chapter 14
1. *Dictionary.com Unabridged (v 1.1)*, s.v.
"Mentor," Dictionary.com, http://dictionary.
reference.com/browse/mentor (accessed
February 23, 2007).
2. *The American Heritage® Dictionary of
the English Language*, 4th edition, s.v.
"Wisdom," Dictionary.com, http://dictionary.
reference.com/browse/wisdom (accessed
February 23, 2007).
3. Max Lucado, *Grace for the Moment*
(Nashville, TN: J. Countryman, Thomas
Nelson, 2000), 66.

Chapter 15
1. *WordNet® 2.1*, s.v. "Fantasy," Dictionary.
com, http://dictionary.reference.com/browse/
fantasy (accessed February 24, 2007).

2. *The American Heritage® Dictionary of
the English Language*, 4th edition, s.v.
"Superhero," Dictionary.com, http://
dictionary.reference.com/browse/superhero
(accessed February 24, 2007).

Chapter 16
1. Dictionary.com. *Kernerman English
Multilingual Dictionary*. K Dictionaries Ltd.
http://dictionary.reference.com/browse/
adventure (accessed: May 04, 2007).
2. http://en.wikipedia.org/wiki/Adventure_
movie.
3. http://www.wayodd.com/184-year-old-
copy-of-the-declaration-of-independence-at-
248/v/6700/
4. *The American Heritage® Dictionary of
the English Language*, 4th edition, s.v.
"Treasure," Dictionary.com, http://dictionary.
reference.com/browse/treasure (accessed
February 26, 2007).
5. Ryan Dobson, *Be Intolerant: Because
Some Things Are Just Stupid* (Sisters, OR:
Multnomah Publishers, 2003), 60.

Chapter 17
1. http://en.wikipedia.org/wiki/Family_film.

Chapter 18
1. http://en.wikipedia.org/wiki/Horror_film.

Chapter 19
1. http://en.wikipedia.org/wiki/Character_arc.

Chapter 20
1. *Dictionary.com Unabridged (v 1.1)*, s.v.
"Climax," Dictionary.com, http://dictionary.
reference.com/browse/climax (accessed
February 27, 2007).
2. *Dictionary.com Unabridged (v 1.1)*, s.v.
"Climax," Dictionary.com, http://dictionary.
reference. com/browse/climax (accessed
February 27, 2007).
3. Max Lucado, *Grace for the Moment*
(Nashville, TN: J. Countryman, Thomas
Nelson, 2000), 268.

Let the Credits Roll
1. *The American Heritage® Dictionary of
the English Language*, 4th edition, s.v.
"Credits," Dictionary.com, http://dictionary.
reference.com/browse/credits (accessed
February 27, 2007).